IMPROVING SALESPEOPLE PERFORMANCE METHODS

JOHN LOK

Contents

Preface

Every organizations need have excellent salespeople to help them to promote their products to sell in order to achieve sale growth. In fact, one supermarket stock keeper or one restaurant waitor, their jobs can be salespeople duty, if one client enquires the stock keeper whether is the food location or any stocks are existence in supermarket. If he can answer enquiries immediately. Then, he can promote the kind of brand food to sell easily. If the restaurant client enquires the waitor that the cooker needs to cook how long time to finish the kind of food, then he can also promote the kind of food to let the client to chooce to eat easily. So, learning salespeople sale psychology and skill , which is important to influence any businesses successes.

In my this book, I shall explain how to know salespeople psychology and every salesperson's strengths or weaknesses of sales skills, in order to find whether whom has which kinds of weaknesses to his/her sale skill to improve. I also indicate any actual business organizations to let readers to evaluate whether their poor sales teams' sale skills , it is one major factor to influence their
long term sale growth in success.

This book concerns my recommendation how entreprensure chooses to achieve whose marketing or/and economy or / and salespeople training strategy to achieve to raise organizational more efficiency and effectiveness. I shall indiate why some UK and US some large business organizations whose weakness and strengths to cause whose organizations inefficient and I shall give recommedation how they can change their marketing or/ and economy or/and human resource (orgnizational behavior) strategy to achieve more efficiency or effectivenss.

This is any salespeople psychological strategy. It concern sample of large companies case studies and indicated how the entrepreneur attempts to apply marketing theoretical bases which are often borrowed from the disciplines of economics and psychology to give opinions to solve these large companies' problems.

Practical application of any salespeople training psycjological strategy theory is provided through case studies. This chapter tries not to present prescriptive solutions to any marketing problems, but encourages discussion about causes and effects. This chapter is arranged in four thematic discussion. The first discussion begins by identifying the fundamental building blocks of marketing. The second thematic discussion focuses on consumers, and on understanding the complex factors that lead to buying decisions. The third thematic discussion focuses on how these sample companies use knowledge about consumers and the broader marketing environment to develop a competitive advantage.

I shall indicate these sample large companies, which had encountered problems do not concern salespeople training strategy what solutions are the best to let them to solve these problems. Thus, these problems were the fact that these sample large companies had encountered. You can learn why these organizations salespeople training strategy is not the major factor to influence their success .

keywords: expectancy theory,ERG theory ,Maslow's Hierarchy ,Concept of motivation ,goal setting theory ,
Attribute theory ,path goal leadership theory ,
organizational cultures and subcultures

Prologue

CONTENTS OF TABLE

CHAPTER ONE

Exciting salespeople performance methods

Any organizations can let salespeople feel happy to sell their products. Then their sale performance will also raise. The question concerns that how to make them to feel happy to help the organization to sell their products? I shall explain some methods as below:

How to manage sales for predictable revenue? In order to hold salespeople sale psychology whether they feel happy or unhappy, executives need to understand the essential activities, sales managers must focus on to be analysts for change, foster continuous improvement and create a sales culture that drives results. Sale executives need to know how to achieve top objectives of sales management is to drive sales, capture new revenue and exceed monthly sales and margin objectives, e.g. performing sale strAregy development with each salesperson on Monday morning at a minimum, and in a formal one-on-one meeting during the week;using strategy tools and questioning techniques to ensure the prospects are qualified and the strategy is valid; knowing the ratio between future values and future monthly quotos to raise sale opportunities; six month on-going sale plan aims to make sure there are coordinated to achieve sale to various market segments; developing on ongoing series of networking events to build market awareness in order to ensure all salespeople attend specific events involved in networking by salespeople to, understanding the market how to influence salespeople sale method to sale number, understanding trends and seeking some channels to raise additional sales opportunities; how to create trained or warm sale environment to let sales teams feel happy to sell.

How to design and utilize efficient control sale procedures? The sale cycle procedure may include these market activities, such as advertising, sales promotion, market research, physical distribution, pricing , sale place, sale staffs seeking. SO, any organizations need

have good sale planning, direction and control of the personnel, selling activities of a business with including recruiting, selecting, training, rating, supervising, paying or reward system, motivating strategy , as all these tasks apply to the personnel sales-force.

The factors may influence salespeople psychology, they may include fair income reward system, or appreciation methods and sale career development plan to every salesperson. It aims to encourage them to achieve the highest sale effort. Anymore, methods to train sale managers have the right direction to guide, lead and motivate their salespeople, e.g. knowledge of salespeople psychology needs how to satisfy them, understanding why they choose to do or act themselves sale behaviors in order to improve their weakness to motivate salespeople to achieve company's sale target goal every month easily, e.g. raising profitability, sales volume, market share, growth and corporate image building raise clients' confidence to choose to buy this company's any products more easily.

The sales organization is required for the following purposes, they may include: enabling top-management, to devote to more time in policy making for the growth and expansion of business to divide and fix authority among the subordinates , so that they may shirk work, to

avoid repetition of duties and functions, so that there may not be any confusion among them to locate responsibility of each and every employee , so that they can complete the whole work in stipulated time, if not then the particular person must be responsible, to establish the sales effort to enforce proper supervision of sales force.

What does the concept of salespeople replacement value mean? What is a sales force turnover management tool? Sales force turnover is defined as the rate at which salespeople leave an organizations, resignations, retirements or dismissals. So, if the organization can raise the sales force turnover ratio, because many salespeople can be promoted or the retirement, or the sales force turnover ratio raising reasons as well as they are not resignation or dismissal reasons. I believe that the organization ought have good sale environment and reasonable reward and welfare strategy to let its salespeople feel happy to help this company to sell its products every day.

However, sales management's actions have direct or indirect effects to impact on turnover. Direct effects may include the firm's firing or dismiss policy. The indirect effects on sale turnover may include new salesperon recruiting and selecting policies affect the quality and performance of the sale force as well as the speed at which salespeople are replaced. The same policies have an impact on the sales force turnover rate through the characteristics of the newly recurited salespersons and the promotion , training, retraining policies, support, supervision, compensation. ALl of those factors have an impact on salesperson's personal satisfaction or dissatisfaction absolutely. So, any sale organizations need to concern how and why whether any one of above these factors may influence their salespeople how to perform or act sale behaviors in order to excite their sale number more effective in long term.

How to achieve sale force management effectively? Sale management is one strategy to many organizations, because organizations expect their salespeople can only raise product sale number. So , they will consider whetther how to implement the sale management strategy to be the most suitable to themselves sale organizations in order to excite their sale teams to sell their products to achieve sale growth aim effectively. So for organization's long term sale growth development, it seems that one excellent sale management strategy can help the organization has stable sale number growth in long term possible.

However, the term " selling" includes a variety of sales situations and activities. For example, those sales positions where the sales representative is required primarily to deliver the product to the customer on a regular or periodic basis. The emphasis is this type of sales activity is very different to the sales position where the sales representative is dealing with sales of capital equipment to industrial purchasers. IN additions some sales representatives deal only in export markets whereas others sell direct to customers in their homes. So, sale organizations need to sell to local or overseas market as well as its target customer is businessmen or individual consumer or both in order to implement to choose their most suitable sale management strategy to train their salespeople more effective or achieving sale growth objective only. Because these its sale major target and where sale market place both factors will influence how it ought train its salespeople, so any organization's training method ought be influenced to change by whom is its major sale target and
where is its major sale market location factors.

How to know the psychology of salesmanship? WHen the organization can predict or find reasons to explain why its salespeople feel unhappy to

help
this organization to sell its products. Then, it can attempt to improve its weaknesses in order to let its salespeople to feel more sale service satisfactory feeling to continue to help this organization to sell its products. THen, it won't need not often to train or recruit new salespeople to replace its old salespeople in consequence. How to know what its salespeoples' real need in order to raise their sale service satisfactory feeling ?

Psychology means that " science of the mind" and psychology plays to important part in business and it is quite worth to bring to influence any organization salespeoples' posivitive or negative sale emotion in their every sale process between themselves and their every client in personal. For example, if the salesperson often have negative emotion or he feels unhappy in every sale process, then he will encounter or increase many times of sale failure possibilities. He will feel that he is one poor verbal advertiser or seller or promotor to help his organization to promote its products to sell again as well as he will lose confidence to sell any products next sale chance, because his failure sale experiences are accumulated to influence his sale emotion to be poor or difficult sale.

Hence, the poor performance salesperson needs have more successful sale experiences to compensate his / her prior many sale failure times feeling, if the organization hopes this poor performance salesperson can raise sale number easily. Overall, any organizations need to concern how to improve or raise the more failure times of sale experience salespeoples' sale techniques or methods or attitudes more than choose to fire or dismiss them as well as finding another new salesperson to replace him/her. Because it is possible that the salesperson 's poor sale performance that is not due to himself/herself poor sale effort and sale knowledge or lacking sale experience to the product, it may be due to the poor sale team cooperation relationship , feeling poor or not comfortable sale physcial shop environment, poor sale manager and other salespeople working relationship, the sale manager lacks leadership effort, poor family relationship etc. external factors more than himself/herself personal poor or negative emotion or poor health etc. personal factors. Hence, the organization ought enquire him/her why he/she feels unhappy to sell its products and it needs to attempt to find methods to solve his/her challenges immediately. If his/her challenges can be solved. It is possible that his/her sale efforts can be also raised for. So, if the organization can know how to utilize positive sale emotion psychological methods to predict or know why and how every salesperson perform his/her sale behavior in whose daily sale tasks, then it can concentrate on implementing effective and the most suitable sale training to raise their sale abilities more easily.

However, the sale training may include: How to build or improve long term good salesperson and his/her customer sale service relationship between every salesperson and every client in every buying and selling cycle process, how to using right communicating styleds for better understanding every client's real needs, powers and negotiating, e.g. every salesperson needs to review why there are many clients do not choose to buy any products from his sale presentation or promotion, finding every time sale failure reasons can let the salesperson makes himself/herself sale failure reasons evaluation or judgement in order to find what is the major reason influences his/her sale failure, e.g. lacking product knowledge, he/she often let many clients to feel that he lacks patience to listen the client's enquiry or feedback, his sale presentation is not attractive to let many clients like to stay longer time to listen his sale presentation in whole sale process, the salesperson himself/herself emotion is negative and he /she can let many clients feel he / she is not happy or does not enjoy to sell this product from himself/herself face impression or sale behavior impression easily, lacking enough sale techniques to persuade his/her clients why he/she ought choose to buy this product in whole sale process etc. these factors may influence the salesperson's sale failure chance to be raised. Hence sales manager ought need to spend long time to meet the poor sale performance salesperson to discuess what his/her sale challenges are the most major to influence his/her every sale successful chance in order to improve his/ her sale performance more successfully.

IN conclusion, the reasons why salespeople often encounter sale failure possibilities. The factors may include these aspects, such as they lask the desire to help customers to make satisfactory purchase decisons, they only concern how to achieve sale final objective or aim only, it will cause clients feel they do not real concern their real needs. They only concern to sell the product in success. They do not know how to describe the product whether what characteristics or features it owns accurately in order to increase sale chance to persudade them to make final decision to by the product, they do not attempt to participate the whole sale process to help them to choose the most right product in order to satisfy their any purcahse needs, they ought avoid deceptive or manipulative influence tactics, avoid the use of high pressure sales techniques etc. Thus, if any organizations can spend time to investigate what factors cause why any one of salespeople choose perform his/her sale behavior often in order to know or understand their salespeople' sale psychology absolutely. Then, I believe that their sale number will only grown more easily.

CHAPTER TWO

Salespeople training strategy is not major successful factor to airline industry

1. If you are the marketing manager of an airline, such as Ryanair, how would you address the ecological concerns?

In recent years, social, economic and environment pressures have pushed airlines to accept their social responsibility. Closely tied to this acceptance is a corporate policy that aims at raising social and environmental standards on a voluntary basis and that means beyond legal and contractual requirement. It means that corporate social responsibility is not just an optional

consideration to core airline business activities, such as airlines industry fuel consumption pollutes sky air to cause global warming problem. Rather, Ryanair airline needs to concern social responsibility because it's fuel emissions would cause negative influence to stakeholders. e.g. causing bad negative climate to influence farmers to grow rice and vegetables etc foods successfully, so global warming will make farmers stakeholder can not earn more income and food buyers stakeholder won't eat rice and vegetables etc. foods easily, even global warming will damage natural environment to cause strong wind or strong raining or water natural hazard to damage any countries' houses to make house owners stakeholder who lose their houses to live. Hence, in the long term, if Ryanair airline still continue consume too much fuels to use to fly to cause emissions to pollute air to any countries as well as other airlines do not achieve any actions to reduce to consume to use more fuels together efficiently. I believe that global warming will become very serious to influence human living and eating problem occurrence in our earth as soon as possibly. Hence, such as Ryanair airline is among of global airlines, which have responsibility to consider how to reduce fuel consumption to cause too much emissions to pollute air in our earth. Such as, I was Ryanair airline marketing manager , I ought need to let Ryanair airline to measure whether it ought only concern how to sell cheaper air fares and buy many airplanes and consume much fuels to fly to raise income or it ought concern it's fuel emissions to pollute environment to cause global warming to influence global human stakeholders encounter living and eating problem to face natural foods resource shortage to supply in the future.

The ecological concerns global warming problem is serious nowadays, it brings the possible long term harmful consequences of executive emissions to the atmosphere. The developed countries, such as Northern Europe and United States people needed often to play travel entertainment by airlines transportation choice. However, scientists proved airlines used fossil fuels to harm excessive emissions to natural environment which would cause global warming problem to cause devastation of low lying areas to influence natural environment danger, even the developing countries people life and their houses would also encountered to be hazarded in the long term. If I was the marketing manager of an airline, such as Ryanair, I must concern socially responsible needs to Ryanair airline. Although, Ryanair aircraft had become more efficient in use of fuel during 1990 years, but Ryanair airline's passengers were booming demand to cause to increase aeroplane numbers to supply to satisfy passengers' travel needs and to pursue raising profit aim every year.

In fact, Ryanair airline used fuels to give energy to push aeroplanes to fly and it also polluted sky air during it's aeroplanes often were flying to cause global warming. For example, Ryanair airline marketing strategy was low fare prices to attract to increase many passengers to choose to attract to increase many passengers to choose to sit it's aeroplanes and it designed a cheap weekend break by Mediterranean travel to increase the unknown and remote possibilities of global warming. Hence, Ryanair would increased many new airplanes to increase to use fossil fuels of excessive emissions to the atmosphere to cause the effects of aid rain, poor climate change , destructive winds, rising sea levels and devastation of low lying areas by global warming bad consequences. Hence, it seemed that Ryanair airline had responsibility to concern how to protect natural environment due to its airplanes numbers and passengers were increasing to cause to increase to use more fossil fuels to cause the possible long term harmful consequences of excessive emissions to the sky to bring global warming occurrence nowadays. As I was this Ryanair airline marketing manager, I shall recommend Ryanair airline needed to consider this global warming socially responsible issue due to its airplanes spent too much fossil fuels to cause harmful consequences of excessive emissions to the sky. It would bring threats to developing countries people life and houses by global warming, so it concerned only how to raise itself interest marketing behavior of performance, but it neglect the serious global warming to cause bad influence to any developing countries people life danger, it was possible that passengers would feel it was not a socially responsible airline company, so it could not build a good image to whom in this airline industry and its further passengers would choose its other competitors (socially responsible airline companies) to substitute its airline service provision.

- Discussion

I should suggest Ryanair airline needed to control fossil fuel numbers to reduce to harm excessive emissions to natural environment seriously and it could spend much expenditure to buy good quality of fossil fuels to active the reduction of too much emissions to damage natural environment aim and it could shorten the sky flying distance to fly to other countries‘ airports from its airport to aim to attempt to reduce to use much fuel to pollute sky air per day and it could cancel some long flight flying routes and increased short flight flying routes to reduce flight spending hours to attempt to reduce to use fossil fuels to provide every airplanes to fly to pollute sky air every day.

Although, these marketing strategies would be possible to reduce airline income, but it would also attract many further passengers to choose to sit to its airplanes to go to travel if it could build good image to prove it was a socially responsible airline to serve passengers to let them to like to choose to use its flying service to go to travel willingly, even it could lead other airlines to follow it to use its marketing strategic methods to reduce to spend too much fossil fuels to pollute sky air to raise global warming problem seriously together. Hence, if Ryanair airline could attempt to achieve to reduce the fossil fuel numbers to use to airplanes to fly , it was possible that the other airline companies should follow it to do the same behaviors to aim to do social responsible organizations to concern how to reduce the global warming problem to cause to harm to our natural environment seriously for long term in the future.

2. The case study refers to apparent hypocrisy of clients who may claim to be concerned about the environment, but nevertheless continue to fly what might bring about a narrowing of this gap between what consumers think and what they actually do?

In fact, some apparent hypocrisy of consumers who may claim to be concerned about the global warming harmful natural environment problem due to airline companies, e.g. Easy Jet,
Ryanair etc. western countries' airlines which allowed fossil fuels produced harmful consequences of excessive emissions to atmosphere, but nevertheless continue to fly. However, I might recommend these methods to bring about a narrowing of this gap between what consumers think and what they actually do.
I think to bring a narrowing of this gap between consumers were happy to carry on airplanes to fly and it would not influence them to concern about climate change problem at the same time.

There was certainly a possible that governments would intervene. Such as the UK government and European commission had floated the idea of taxing aviation fuel and brought aircraft emissions within scope of the European emission trading scheme. Thus, if these western countries governments raised to charge aviation fuel taxing, it would possible to threaten any western airlines to shorten any flight routes hours and flight flying distance to fly to destination of the countries' airports from these airline companies' every country's airport, so which would not need to use more fuels for its airplanes to use if it had shorten flight flying routes distance to arrive other countries' airports. Hence, the airlines did not want to pay higher aviation tax to government, so which would attempt to shorten some flight flying routes from long distance to be short distance when their airplanes needed to fly to some other countries' airport to aim to buy less fuel numbers or which would not buy more airplanes.

Due to they needed to pay high aviation tax expenditure to their countries governments every year. Thus, it was possible that high fuel tax expenditure would cause airlines to shorten flight routes time. The most important, when some airlines decided to buy less fuels. These airlines might bring about a narrowing of this gap between what consumers think and what they actually do and these airlines were possible to raise their competitive ability, due to which would possible to persuade the concerned environment protective passengers who would choose to buy these airlines air tickets to more than to buy the other airlines‘ air tickets. Due to some airlines could not reduce to buy more fuel numbers to provide their airplanes to fly and which would increase air pollution to sky seriously, those airlines' spending excessive long hours (time) of every flight flying routes to fly to different countries‘ airports which would use more fuel to fly to cause air pollution to harm natural environment seriously and which would let these clients to feel unhappy to choose to buy air tickets to sit their airplanes possibly. Hence, different governments raised aviation tax would cause many airlines to reduce to buy too much fuel numbers to use possibly. It seemed that airlines needed have a social responsible duty to concern they needed to buy more fuels if they increased airplanes numbers, then they would raise air pollution to cause global warming problem seriously. Hence, I think passengers would not buy air tickets to fly to travel by airplanes when who would have long days of holidays. Otherwise, who would choose to stay at home or who would choose to go to travel by cruises on water transportation on their holidays. However, in western developed economies, legislation to enforce environmentally sensitive methods of productive is increasing, so airlines might adopt environmentally sensitive flight service processes to gain a competitive advantages. The challenges of using fuels resources in more efficient and less polluting way has achieved research and development, e.g. wind power research, solar panels, heat pumps and carbon capture technology have presented opportunities for airlines to improve the efficiency of fuels and airline marketing to business and individual group passengers.

Legal actions to place control over the emission of air pollutants have been instituted in several ways, such as the form of a public nuisance low. This is when conditions cause discomfort, inconvenience, damage to property or injury from airlines fuels to cause air pollution. The governments have also intervened in the protection of the public to threaten the airlines' fuels emissions pollute air in the sky. As a result of much research, devices for pollution control have been developed, guidelines for air quality were established fuels tax increasing incentives were introduced to enforce ordinances for restricting the emission from airplanes‘ fuels. For example, governments can pass the clean air act, legislation to reduce air pollution in their countries. In conclusion, airlines can co-operate environmentally friendly management to prevent global warming, it is as a part of its corporate social responsibility and makes company wide efforts to do by saving energy and reducing aircraft fuel emissions. Hence, global airlines ought plan to achieve to reduce to consume excessive fuel emissions to reduce a narrowing of this gap between what consumers think and what they actually do concerned about the environment pollution was caused by airlines if which still wanted to make travelers who prefer to choose to go to travel by flying more than other water or ground transportation etc. methods.

3. How would a company , such as Easy Jet airline measure and monitor consumer's attitudes?

Easy Jet airline has created environment problems, e.g. harmful chemicals sift down from smoky trails of low-flying jets. The scream of Easy Jet airline engines is constantly heard by

people who love near big city airports. It's aircrafts produce air pollution with consequent changes in climate.

It is a fact that many people prefer air travel rather than ground or water transportation, This has promoted a critical look at safety and quality control. Contributions to air pollution is a chief concern because of this revolutionary change in public transportation in the United States and around the world. The government must also establish standards for exhaust emissions. Thus, Easy Jet airline measure and monitor consumer's attitudes which needs to indicate to let them to believe that which suggests which airplane manufacturers are forced to develop low pollutant engines.

Due to the problem of air pollution from its airplanes involve a complex set of interactions among technical, social and economic factors. Hence, it also needs to measure it's emission from Easy Jet aircrafts, particularly on landing and take offs, are a source of bitter complaints from nearby residents. In a few airports visibility has been dangerously restricted by particulate emissions and photo chemical smog. Easy Jet airline also needed to have energy savings activities to its operations, ranging from procedural and flight plan improvement to reduce flight distance and attitude and weight management and it also needed to create energy through maintenance to achieve to continue to reduce co2 emissions by introducing high efficiency aircraft and through other measures to monitor consumers' attitudes . In line with its aim to be an environmentally friendly airline that harmonizes the needs of natural , humans and airline businesses. It aims to be respected by society , live up to its social responsibilities and make a contribution to society. Although emissions from aircraft are not included among greenhouse gas reduction targets, but it also needed to make systematic efforts to improve energy efficiency and reduce emissions by creating a road map to actively participate . Furthermore, Easy Jet airline also needed continually to pursue a management style that concerns nature, people and fellow corporations, even under the most severe conditions as a major practice toward implementing its environmental policy. Easy jet airline achieves environment goals to measure and monitor consumer's attitudes, such as minimizes energy and resource consumption and introduces up to date and fuel efficient fleet and engines and develops and apply energy efficient operation technique, it establish strict internal environmental standards to set internal standards that are stricter than general environment laws applied worldwide and minimize pollutants through systematic management and observance of standards. It systematically analyses the airlines' environmental impact and make the outcome to carry out reductions and evaluates the environmental impact of its aviation operations, maintenance and service and improves environmentally friendly processes and it continually improves environmental systems through feedback .

In conclusion, Easy Jet airline can increase the recycling of waste to reduce fuel consumption of resources and it can make systematic efforts to reduce emissions by creating a roadmap and actively participating in global warming by saving energy and reducing aircraft emissions through engine washing to aim to consume fuels efficiency and reduce emission to pollute air.

4. What might be the consequences for the marketing of a budget airline of Government policy measures which have the effect of doubling air fares in real terms?

If the country Government decided to raise higher flight fuel tax charge policy to budget airline. Due to the country Government hoped budget airline to reduce fuels consumption to provide to airplanes to use to reduce sky air pollution to cause global warning problem. In fact, budget airline needed to increase to use much fuels to provide to many flights to carry on passengers travel needs. Generally, budget airline would not like to choose to reduce to consume much fuels due to it's passenger numbers had been increasing. If budget airline decided to buy less fuels to reduce much fuels to consume for its flight needs. It would lose many passengers if it had not enough times of flights to provide airplanes to fly to different countries' airports to satisfy passengers' different flight route choices. However, the consequences for budget airline would also be passengers to choose to buy budget airline air tickets possibly if it decided to raise doubling air fares in real terms. Due to budget airline hoped to compensate its loss if it's country Government raised higher fuels tax to cause budget airline needed to pay high cost expenditure every year. Hence, budget airline needed to raise to spend two kinds of expenditure every year, such as purchasing more fuels expenditure and paying more fuels expenditure both. For long term, budget airline would choose to raise doubling or more air fairs in real terms in order to reduce to need to pay too much feel tax expenditure to compensate it's loss every year. In result, it's passengers would feel it's air tickets fares were not reasonable raised to compare it's other airline competitors, but it's flight services were not excellent to compare it's airline competitors specially. Hence, it's increasing air fares would cause many passengers to choose other airline competitors possibly.

5. Critically discuss how the marketing manager of a budget airline might respond.

Marketing manger might use cost benefit analysis to let budget airline to know how to invest in intangible asset, such as corporate social responsibility to give long term benefit to itself budget airline. I suggest this marketing manager needs to explain the reason why reducing fuel consumption is an investment in intangible asset to budget airline as below: Airline transport has increasingly become a global technologically and dynamic growth industry. However, airline companies need to remain committed to satisfy the clients' growing demands in a sustainable manner when at the same time maintaining an optimal balance between economic progress, social development and environmental responsibility. The concept of corporate social responsibility is a challenge for who to face today's risky, competitive and complex airline business environment. There has been a need for airlines in the airline industry to develop an environment agenda and take measures to minimize the ever increasing environmental impacts created by their activities. The forms of corporate social responsibility in the airline sector includes working in partnership with local communities, socially sensitive investment as well as involvement in activities for conservation of the environment. The fact, airlines are spewing 20% more co2 into the environment then previously estimated and there is a tendency for amount to increase to 1.5 billion tons a year by 2025 year. So, airline industry must need to innovative, environmentally responsible industry that drives economic and social progress. It has risks (social, environmental, operational, threat, strategic and financial risks) that they have to deal with marketing managers airlines, such as budget airline marketing manager is responsible for the optional decision making about corporate risks in its daily business. Adrian, (P. 2012) indicated that the marketing manager of budget airline needs to indicate the benefits can be categorized into three namely to let budget airline to feel as below:

(a) Regarding the economic view, budget airline is essential for facilitating world business and tourism, it needs to create jobs and enables the expansion of trade across the global by opening
up new market opportunities. It also attracts businesses to locations all over the world, hence satisfying the mobility requirement of a growing portion of the world's population. It also aids in the movement of products and services quickly over long distance facilities economies and social participation by remote communities.

(b) From the social perspective, budget airline forms an unique global transport network that links people in different countries safely and efficiently. Air transport is increasingly accessible to a large number of people who can now afford to travel by air for pleasure and its business purpose.

(c) Lastly, in terms of the environmental perspective, there is a need for budget airline to minimize or contain the impact in its environment through the continuous improvement of its
fuel consumption, noise reduction and the introduction of new technologies. Budget airline marketing manager can enquire this question to whose company, such as how budget airline can quantify the benefits derived from such investments to do with how to quantify the benefits, so budget airline can be compared to the cost of investments. Through budget airline has be different over the years to value many intangibles, such as corporate social responsibilities. Budget airline marketing manager needs to make choices among several alternatives: it is important to adopt a tool that with allow choices to clearly weigh and distinguish between the options available. So, budget airline marketing manager needs to persuade whose company to believe to maximize the gain, which may be either economic or social and may be beneficial to an individual, a group or society at large, e.g. reducing fuel cost can maximize economic or social benefits for long term. The measurement of benefits from corporate social responsibility policy includes gains from additional income to an increased quality of life or a cleaner environment.

On the other hand, the costs are made up of the opportunities forgone, internal and external costs and externalities. For instance, increasing the flying route for budget airline, the noise and air pollution are the externality when the secondary effect could be an increase in the cost operations. In this case, the pollution creates the new cost (externality). The budge airline business cost is the increase in the cost of operating the additional route. The budget airline's fuel consumption causes air pollution will influence whose client stakeholders' powers of seeing and thinking, cultural setting, experience is from the past and motivation at the time of sensing to the airline image to be poor due to who will feel the budget airline is not a social responsible organization. It aims to earn profits from passengers, but it neglects to take care other stakeholders benefits due to its fuel consumption to pollute environment to cause global warming problem. It seems that budget airline needs to considerate to use more fuel consumption to cause global warming problem more than doubling air fares in real terms if Government decided to raise more fuel tax charging to it to reduce its income.

I suggest marketing manager of a budget airline to reduce to use more fuels to pollute air, so budget airline does not decide to increase double air fairs charges to clients due to Government raises fuel taxation expenditure. Because it will cause clients to cancel its air tickets if who feel its air fairs are not reasonable to raise prices to compare other airline competitors. The marketing manager of a budget airline might respond to promote this navigation system to persuade budget airline does not choose to double air fares if Government raised fuel taxing charge. Innovation of flight operation on the optimum routes using (RNAV) Area navigation, as conventional airways and routes between airports were built by connecting ground navigation aids to the destination, the budget airline often became rather inefficient. On the other hand, RNAV can build routes connected any points with almost straight line by confirming aircraft position by means of global positioning system etc in addition to radio navigation destination of fuel consumption and CO2 emission through shortened flight time and distance. Other reducing fuel consumption include reduction of aircraft weight, use of new type point for aircraft painting to reduce emission of polluted to air . Hence, budget airline will spend less fuels to avoid to pay high fuels taxation expenditure to its Government and it does not need to charge double air fairs in real terms to cause many passengers who will choose to find other airlines to buy cheaper air tickets or who will cancel their budget airline air tickets due to who feel budget airline charges unreasonable air fairs. So, if budget airline did not achieve as above any methods to attempt to reduce fuel consumption, I believe that it will lose many passengers due to it decide to charge doubling air fares in real terms to compensate its fuel tax increasing expenditure .

CHAPTER THREE

Salespeople training strategy is major successful factor to sport shoe industry

1. How can ethnographic research predict consumer emotion ?

Critically assess the role of ethnographic research as a means of learning More about buyer behavior. To critically assess whether the role of ethnographic research as a means of learning more about buyer behavior. I shall indicate what the marketers who use general methods to learn more about buyer behavior to compare to ethnographic research difference. In general, marketers learn buyer behavior who shall follow the simplified stages in the buyer decision process , such as the beginning is from need recognition to information search to evaluate to decision to the end of post purchase evaluation stage. Hence, the any buyers behavior shall be cycle stage to decide whether who shall repeat to choose to buy the company's product or use it's service if who feel the product or service had achieved their satisfaction after who spent. The marketers shall use questionnaires or marketing researches to enquire consumers to gather their ideas to analysis to get evaluation to assess whether how whose companies need to produce what kinds of new products style, design, color, price level and sale channels to achieve the most suitable marketing strategy to raise their sale competition. Otherwise, the role of ethnographic search is one different method to learn more about buyer behavior. In general, companies shall not need to arrange questionnaires to enquire participants to fill to answer questions to gather data to carry on evaluation and which do not need to follow the simplified stages to assess target client groups purchase decision process to carry on the sale and post purchase evaluation cycle to evaluate whether what are their product criteria or weaknesses which need to improve to raise their sale competition in their market. I think ethnographic research can get closer to the truth about consumer behavior. On behalf of companies' clients, which can seek to uncover hidden truths about the way their clients' lead their lives, by paying volunteers to be followed for days on end, being filmed and having their every more recorded. Companies will pay their target householder participant group to carry on an observational survey by digital cameras to be filmed record at home. One essential feature of ethnographic research is that it must not have any predetermined agenda.

There is little value in undertaking this type of research if the mind set of the researcher is expecting to see preconceived phenomena, it is the unexpected that is often of most interest, and which is so difficult to pick up through more structured forms of survey. In fact, participants in a survey may feel self conscious when who are being filmed, and the more interesting insights are likely to be observed when participants are feeling relaxed and off their guard .It is not just what people actually do that can be interesting, but what they almost do, and the body language used when members of the household are discussing an issue. It can take several hours of filming to yield just a few moments of true insights into participants' true attitudes and behavior.

One example of the company's ethnographic research in action was provided by a project commissioned by the footwear brand Dr Martens. It wanted to understand how young people used fashion brands in their every lives . Why for example, did some brands, such as Nike trainers or baseball caps become popular in youth culture? The researchers identified groups of young people around the world who responded to Dr Martens' target market. In return for a payment, volunteers were followed for several days and their daily routines filmed with a handheld digital camera. In total, 180 hours of captured film was edited to just one hour of highlights showing the key drivers of youth culture which are relevant to the Dr Martens brand. It seemed that young people preferred fashions that allowed them to customize an item of clothing and in some way take ownership of it. The research drew the conclusion that iconic fashion items for young people had to have a distinctive label or style that made their wearers stand out as part of a tribe. Hence, ethnographic research seems to help this company to know why the young clients choose to buy other brand sport shoes, it is possible that they the other brands sport shoes' color or design can be accepted more to than to buy Dr Marten brand's sport shoes when they wear different style of clothing. Hence, it can use digital camera to observe the worldwide choice of paying target youth volunteers whose daily individual behaviors at homes to get the more actual evidence to evaluate what factors influence youth clients choose to buy other brands of sport shoes. Otherwise, if it use structured questionnaire surveys to enquire youth clients , it is possible that who can not give their feedbacks honestly. Otherwise, observable youth people whose daily activities can help this company to know it is possible that their design and color of clothing are one factor to influence their choice to buy preferable brands of sport shoes to wear if who felt the brand of sport shoe was suitable to wear to influence their clothing to be felt more smart in appearance. However, I suggest companies to avoid to tell householders what the research project is about, until it is over. That way, the chances of participants deliberately playing to the camera can be reduced.

Hence, ethnographic researcher ought not tell to participants why who needs to record their daily activities at home till to the end of observable survey finishing due to it is possible that the participants will not perform their actual behaviors if who knew the researcher's observable intention. However, if marketers need to understand how whose companies clients actually make purchase decisions to their products, who shall use structured questionnaire surveys for collecting large scale factual data, but it will have major weaknesses when companies can not understand individual's attitude. Complex sets of factors that influence their buying decisions can only rarely be captured by a questionnaire.

Qualitative approaches such as those using focus groups can get closer to the truth, but participants often still find themselves inhibited from telling the full story to the companies to know.

Ethnography is one of many approaches that can be found within social research. Ethnography was a descriptive account of a community or culture. Ethnography usually involves the researcher participating in people's daily lives for an extended

period of time, watching what happens, listening to what is said, and/or asking questions through informal and formal interviews collecting documents. In more detailed terms, ethnographic work usually has most of the following features: People actions are studied in every contexts rather than under conditions created by the researcher, such as in experimental setups or highly structured interview situations as well as data are gathered from a range of sources including documentary evidence of various kinds, but participant observation and/or relatively informal conversations are usually the main ones as well as data collection is for the most past relatively unstructured in two senses and it doesn't involve following through detailed research design at the start and the categories that are used for interpreting what people say or do are not built into the data collection process through the use of observation schedules or questionnaire to analysis.

Generally, fairly small scale, perhaps a single setting or group of people. This is a facilitate in depth study and the analysis of data involves interpretation of the meanings, functions and consequences of human actions and how these are implicated in local and perhaps also wider contexts what are produced for the most part are verbal descriptions, explanations and theories and statistical analysis play a subordinate role at most. How ethnography can learn more about buyer behavior. It means collection of data to pursue an answers to these questions more effectively and to test these against evidence. Collecting data in natural settings, in other words in those that have not been specially set up for research purposes (such as experiments or formal interviews). Where participant observation is involved the researcher must have some role in the studied and this

will usually have to be done at least through implicit and probably also through explicit, negotiation with people.

The methodological model for social research is physical science conceived in terms of the logic of the experiment. Ethnography was sometimes dismissed as quite inappropriate to social science on the grounds that the data and findings it produces are subjective. Hence, ethnographic research is the role to learn more about buyer behavior through marketers may have been listening more to consumers (e.g. through qualitative research), efforts have almost always been directed at controlling consumers; ranges of products or services pre determined by producers have been pushed through with little real involvement of consumers in the process at a time in which consumers are ever more aware of what is being done to marketers. Ethnographic field research involves the study of groups and people as who go about every day lives. There has two distinct activities. First, the ethnographer enter into a social setting and gets to know the people involved in it; who participates in the daily routines; develops ongoing relations with the people in it and observes all the approach. But second the ethnographer writes down in regular systematic ways what who observes and learns when participating in the daily rounds of life of others. Thus, the researcher creates an accumulating written record of these observations and experiences. These two interconnected activities comprise the core of ethnographic search: firsthand participation in some initially unfamiliar social world and the production of written accounts of that world by drawing upon such participation. Hence, ethnographers are committed to get close to the activities and everyday people.

Getting close minimally requires physical and social proximity to the daily rounds of people's lives and activities, the field researcher must be able to take up positions in the midst of the key sites and scenes of other's lives in order observe and understand whom. In learning about others through active participation in their lives and activities. Finally, close continuing participation in the lives of others encourages appreciation of social life as ongoing processes. Through participation the field researcher sees how people do uncertainty and confusion, how meaning is through talk and collective action, how understandings change over time.

Consumer behavior refers to the behavior that consumers display in searching for purchasing, using, evaluating and disposing of products and services that who expect will satisfy their needs and it's behaviors that are directly involved in the action of obtaining, consuming and spending products/services, including the decision processes that precede and follow these actions. The knowledge of consumer behavior helps the marketer to understand how consumer think, feel and select from alternative like products, brands and the like and how the consumers' buying behaviors are influenced by their environment, the reference groups, family and salespersons. Most of the factors are uncontrollable and beyond the controls of marketers, but who have to be considered when trying to understand the complex behavior of the consumers. Consumers buying cycle processes involved when individuals or groups select, purchase, use or dispose of products or services or ideas or experiences to satisfy needs and desires.

In the marketing context, the term consumer refers not only to the act of purchase itself, but also to patterns of aggregate buying which include pre-purchase and post purchase activities.

Pre-purchase activity might consist of the growing awareness of a need or wants and a search for and evaluate of information about the products and brands that might satisfy it. Post purchase activities include the evaluation of the purchased item in use and the reduction of any anxiety which accompanies the purchase of expensive and infrequently bought items. The various factors include lifestyles and its impact on the consumer behavior. On the first hand, ethnographic research can learn more about buyer behavior as below: ethnographic research described the dominant, positivistic consumer perspectives and methodological and analytical overview of the traditional perspectives. There are two factors mainly influencing the consumers for decision making. Risk aversion and innovativeness. Risk aversion is a measure of how much consumers need to be certain and sure of what who are purchasing. Highly risk adverse consumers need to be very certain about what who are buying. Whereas less risk adverse consumers on tolerate some risk and uncertainty in their purchasing. The second variable, innovativeness is a global measure which captures the degree to which consumers are willing to take chances and experiment with new ways of doing things. Hence, ethnographic research can learn whether the buyer's shopping motivation is abound with which various measures of individual characteristics, e.g. innovative, variety seeking etc. different factors to the buyer behavior.

On the second hand, perception is a mental process, whereby an individual selects data or information from the environment organizes it and then draws significance or meaning from it. Perceived fit is an attitudinal measure of how appropriate a certain channel of distribution is for a specific product. Consumer's perception of the fit between a service/ product and channel is very influential in determining whether who will consider using that channel for a specific service. In fact, perceived fit was found to be more important than consumer's preference for the distribution method or service. Product quality and packaging and brand awareness familiarity with a channel is a measure of the general experience who have with purchasing products through special channels , e.g. internets, newspapers advertisement factors let consumers to decide to choose to buy or not buy the specific product. Shopping motives are defined as consumer's wants and needs as who relate to outlets at which to shop. Two groups of motives, functions and non functional have been proposed with time, place and possession needs and refer to rational aspects of channel choice. The functional motives included convenience, price comparison. Otherwise, the non functional motives entailed recreation and it related to social and emotional reasons. Hence, ethnographic research can assess whether the product or service is the functional motive or non functional motive to cause the buyer's choice.

On the third hand, economic theory holds that of largely rational and conscious economic calculations. Thus, the individual buyer seeks to spend whose income on those products that will deliver the most utility (

satisfaction) according to his tastes and relative prices. It aimed to simplify assumptions and examine the effects of changes in single variables (e.g. price) holding all other variables constant. (e.g. low price of product is the higher the sales. The identified the impact of price differentials on consumers' brand preferences; changes in produces on demand variations; changes in price on demand sensitivity and scarcity on consumer choice behavior amongst many others. The consumer behavioral perspective in contrast to the economic view which underscores the importance of internal processes in consumer decision making, the behavioral perspective emphasizes the role of external environmental factors in the process of learning, when which it is argued causes behavior. The behavioral perspective therefore focuses on external environmental, such as advertisement that stimulate consumer response through learning. Consumers must be exposed to information, e.g. advertisement of it is to influence their behavior. Hence, ethnographic research can assess whether the product/service is consumer behavioral perspective or behavioral perspective to cause the buyer's choice.

On the fourth hand, consumers were suggest that high involvement with a product results in an extended problem followed by an information search, alternative evaluation, purchase and post purchase activities. The process is aided by an active information processing sequence involving exposure, attention, comprehension, acceptance and retention. The choice is determined by the outcome of the information process aided decision sequence may have satisfying or dissatisfying outcomes. Consumer's motivation and intention and that unpredictable factors (such as non availability brand or insufficient funds) may result in modification of the actual choice made by a consumer. This model assumes that observed consumer behavior is preceded by intrapersonal psychological states and events (attitude intention-purchase sequence). Hence, the events are as outputs of the processing of information, taking for granted that consumers seek and use information as part of their rational problem solving and decision making processes. Hence, ethnographic research can learn why the buyer doesn't choose to buy the product whether it is unpredictable or predictable psychological factors.

On the fifth hand, personality perspective means some purchases have more personal relevance than others. When this partly reflects on factors, such as price, it also bears on the way in which some products enhance the consumer's self concept , e.g. possessions are considered to reflect on a consumer's image of whom. Personality in general is understood as a concept. Personality has also been understood as the unique way in which traits, attitudes, when individuals might not always be uniform and predictable in their patterns of choice in different situations, it might be possible to make sense of and to forecast the general reactions of broadly defined groups and classes of purchasers.

It is the concept of consumer general behavioral response patterns that forms the basis for marketing's personality based segmentation strategies. The possibility of using measures of personality to guide marketing action, for example in segmenting markets , tailoring new brands of innovative consumers and repositioning mature brands has encouraged a large volume of research. Attitude itself is a learning experience and can lead to a change in attitudes before buyers enter the buying process. Thus, attitudes don't automatically guarantee all types of behavior. They are really the product of social forces interacting with the individual's unique temperament and abilities and social influences are not all of the behavioral variations in people. Two individuals subject to the same influences are not likely to have identical attitudes, although those attitudes will probably more points than those of two and cognition. Affect refers to the way a consumer feel about an attitude object, behavior involves the person's intentions to do something with regard to an attitude object and finally cognition refers to the beliefs a consumer has about an attitude object.

Thus, ethnographic research can learn whether it is from external social factors more or internal personality factors more to cause the buyer's choice. The theory of cognitive information processing , attitudes are formed in the order of beliefs, affect and behavior. Attitudes based on behavioral learning follow the beliefs, behaviors and affect sequence and finally attitudes formed based on the experiential hierarchy follow the affect, behavior and beliefs route. A consumer who is highly involved with a product / service category and who perceives a high level of product/ service differentiation between alternatives will follow the cognitive hierarchy (beliefs affect behavior). From the ethnographic research marketers perspective the sequence of attitude formation is from a communication point of views from a strategic point of view, such as it has proved useful in specifying the different elements that work together to influence buyers' evaluations of attitudes ; products or services may be composed of many attributes or qualities, some of which may be more important than others to particular people. So consumer's decision is to act on whose attitude is affected by other factors, such as whether it is felt other factors, such as whether it is felt that buying a product/ service would be met with approval by friends and family. The complexity of attitudes is underscored by multi attribute attitude models, in which sets of beliefs and evaluations are identified and combined to predict an overall attitude.

On the final hand, the situational influence perspective, a situation is defined by factors over and above the characteristics of a person and product or service. For example, situational affects may be behavioral (e.g. entertaining friends), experiential or perceptual (e.g. being depressed or being pressed for time). According to the behavioral influence perspective of low involvement decision situation, consumer decision making is a learned response to environmental cues, as when a person decided to buy something on impulse that is prompted as a surprise special in a store.

According to this approach, then ethnographic research marketers must concentrate on assessing the characteristics of the environment, such as the physical surroundings and product/service placement, that influence members of that target market. For example, point of purchase (such as product/ service samples) are particularly useful in inducing impulse purchases. Ethnographic research marketers focus on measuring consumers' effective responses to products or services and develop offerings that elicit appropriate subjective reactions and employ effective symbolism. Situational effects can also be perceptive, e.g. there could be a number of ways in which mood can influence purchase decisions. For example, stress can impact information processing and problem solving abilities. In addition, time poverty can impact buying decisions. An individual's priorities determine whose time style. According, consumer buying change is not something which consumers do for themselves, rather it is a result of something that is done to them by some internal ,e.g. trait or external ,e.g. environment force over which they have little or no control. Thus, ethnographic research can assess what is the situational influence factors to cause the buyer to choose to buy the product or consume the service. In conclusion, conditions of competition are changing rapidly today and companies need strategies to react to those changes promptly to raise competition. Due to technological developments, physical differences of products/ services have decreased. Differentiation should be on the meanings products/
services bear instead of on their physical features and a successful brand differentiation can be possible by building personality. Hence,

understanding consumer behaviors are related to marketing natures in the product sale or service provision to every marketer who needs to considerate to win whose competitors.

2. Discuss the ethical issues that are raised by ethnographic research.

Consumer research has been important to the development of marketing theory and practice. Consumers are seldom, if ever, involved in the research design and analysis processes which raises issues that go beyond ethics. Particularly, problematic when participant observation is employed , as little is and little could be addressed by research guidelines and codes of ethics relevant to marketing research. Some of the relevant ethical issues to participant observation that arise from the lack of the consumer in the research process as well as the potential issues that may be involved in participatory research designs, the shortcomings of the available ethnographic marketing research guidelines and codes of ethics as for as participant observation is concerned. Some argument regards the real time and nature of ethical circumstances at the field where the ethnographic researcher must often respond to unexpected situations immediately.

3. Why ethical ways of thinking it is important to recognize that are raised by ethnographic research.

It is possible that the issues of power that can arise ethnographic research as well as it is from the consequences of simply doing research , even if the intentions are good and it is from the fact that ethnographic research marketers' knowledge system is necessarily linked to other forms of structural power (e.g. gender, race, development, the system). The ethnographic research marketers whose emotional and power issues present in ethnographic research relationships are also acknowledged to influence ethnographic results, and this is where the key issues of using research participants for data collection comes in. Ethnographic research designs that objectify and don't include research participants in the conceptualization of the research study through to data analysis have been widely criticized by ethnographic researchers and these issues must be considered within the scope of the ethics of care.

Researchers (ethnographers) need have moral responsibilities toward research, included informed consent, confidentiality, reliability and validity. In sum, ethical guidelines and codes of conduct can be beneficial in alerting consumer researchers of ethical ways of conducting research. However, participants needed rules to be aided by researchers' own ethical reasoning in the field. The ethnographic researchers need to highlight the importance of constant negotiation of participation in the different stages of research, how participants may not be willing (due to lack of time or even personal circumstances) to help ethnographic researchers in the data analysis process and how researchers' own deadlines and academic constraints may get in the way of the idealized research process of involvement between ethnographic research participants and researchers are well to their discussed topic. In general, ethnographic researchers need to know what who need to understand about ethics, such as harm, consent, data protection etc. recap of ethical approval what it is and what ethnographic researchers need to do and what further sources of information and support need.

In ethic principles, ethnographic research should be designed, reviewed and undertaken to ensure integrity and quality. Participants must normally be informed fully about the purpose, methods and intends possible uses of research, what their participation entails and what risks, the confidentiality must be respected research participants must take part voluntarily, harm to research participants must be avoided in all instances and the independence of research must be clear and any conflicts to interest or partiality must be explicit and increasing stakeholder demands. The mature of the ethical consumer is educated, middle class or over emotional to decide what kind products who needs to buy and how many numbers are enough to buy. For example, with the environment dropping out of media attention, ethic provided new moral ground and campaigns or opening of a chain of ethical supermarkets, ethical image became a desirable commodity for the big retailers. Some ethical customers need to satisfy with fair trade marked products to buy from the ethical supermarkets. How morality may play a significant role in the performance of buyers' actions. It is concerned specifically with how rules, responsibilities and values centering on right or wrong influence the character of consumption. The idea that morality (ethicality) can have a considerable impact upon the consumption. Hence, I think business moral performance is needed to satisfy every buyer's decision of consumption and it is linked to the ethnographic research growing literature on ethical consumer behavior. Within psychology, for instance, morality can be seen as a process of cognitive learning where systematic punishment and reward help to educate individuals of their actions. Whether consumption is informed by at least some of the available moral perspectives to some of the available moral perspectives, so it caused ethical issues that are raised by ethnographic research. Ethical consumption is concerned with predicting market behavior, it included some kind of relationship between the attitudes, values and behaviors of a defined ethical consumer group. For example, ethnographic researchers have been interested in the effects of environmental concern on environmentally friendly consumer behavior. Depending on how ethical consumption is defined, it recognizes alternative forms of what are essentially moral values, attitudes and buyer individual behavior. Consumer behavior has been changed by external elements, such as economy, technology, cultures, religion etc. factors. It would be unfortunate to be great importance for an understanding of ethical consumption issues.

In conclusion, consumption behavior is the art of need for desire to, it could be thought of as directly influenced by certain core values held as sacred within society. For example, ethical buyer behavior may concerns about animal protection, environmental protection, human protection etc. life rights issue. Facts, knowledge and truth about morality in consumption are seen as being raised by ethnographic research. According, the relationship between morality and consumers behavior could be better through of as the products of a continued process of political, social, technological and religious re-organization of life. For example, capabilities of new digital , microchip technology enhanced many consumers with the delights of efficient, task-saving, small and shiny products. Simultaneously, and not unrelated turbo-charges cars, mobile phones, cock tail parties etc. high technological products are arguably reflected power, success and good living to influence buyer behavior ethically daily in our society. Hence, I believe ethical issues that are needed to consider by ethnographic research.

4. Discuss possible alternative approaches by which marketers may learn more about youth culture.

Market based trading -selling, buying and consuming has existed in our society. Human action and interaction and behaving in different roles in exchange markets and various trading situations which is a typical of consumers and market trading interplays of several actors in economic, societal and cultural contexts as well as consumer behavior and consumer culture and consumption which have close relationship. Individual youth consumer or a group of youth consumers who is described as humanistic economics where people, their values and culture are primarily analyzed. In general, research on brands and organizational issues of the marketing function defined the questions of how to sell more products or provide more services to speed up the general level of consumption in order to

better the economic situation of a firm or a nation. Basically, individual youth buyer seeks to speed whose income on those products/services what will deliver the most utility, typically satisfaction, according to whose tastes and budget. In economic, consumer behavior is identified with rational decision making. Decisions are automatically translated into purchasing and consuming, The price and income constraints are generally accepted factors in an economic analysis of
consumer behavior. Consequently, consumers are seen as rational actors that purposefully optimize the production of their utility.

Sociological and macro and cultural perspective which focuses on consuming , emphasizes on emotions, multicultural new consumers aspects, cultural studies and the meaning of culture for consumer research surfaced also in the late 1980 years. For example, consumption symbolism, different aspects to property and possessions, political consumption, research and cultures and subcultures. In consumer studies can be traced to the mid 1990 years, when consumer culture was recognized as a distinct cultural entity. Consumption was seen as a society activity which above all others, unities economy and culture. The one alternative approach is that learning more about youth culture, there is a clear common sense about its influence on social youth consumption changes, and the importance of its analysis in order to understand modern youth consumption. For example, marketers may learn more how to make youth to cause excessive consumption nowadays. The influence of the means of mass communication and oriented medias has contributed to send promotion messages to different youth audiences, e.g. from children and teen ages to youths. To see themselves in real conditions why who need to buy products or need services before beyond their possibilities have been planned to buy electronics, cars and even a house etc. products.

The another alternative approach is that marketers may also learn what are youth consumer modern culture how to make them, such as symbol status and power how become habituated to consume familiar products/ services able to reinforce familiar image in youth cultural different target groups. The final alternative approach is that culture is sociological influence on client's needs, it is based on the individual's physiological and psychological needs, such as food choice. Maslow recognized that once individual have satisfied these basic physiological needs, such as foods and drinks, who may seek to satisfy social needs by cultural influence, for example, the need to have meaningful interaction with peers. More complex still, western cultures see increasing numbers of people seeking to satisfy essentially internal needs for self satisfaction, products therefore satisfy increasing complex needs. Moreover, food is no longer seen as a basic necessary to be purchased and cooked for self consumption with growing prosperity, youth people have sought to satisfy social needs by eating out with friend or family. Youth peoples' satisfaction of such social needs may influences on their foods sating basic needs. Hence, if the youth clients had afford to go to restaurant to eat more expensive and good taste foods. The high class food culture can change the youth client's food necessity to influence whose food choice. A young child is often considered society unacceptable, so such youth behavior is socialized out before the child reaches adulthood. The faculty cultural influences a child's perception of the world and the family cultural influences lasts into adulthood. For example of this effect on buying processes can be found in youth adults selection of a particular brand breakfast cereal because it is the one that who were brought up with youth individuals are surrounded by peer group/or reference groups with act as a guide for youth consumption of behavior peer groups can be primary and direct to influence their youth culture (e.g. colleagues at work and school), popular movie actors can secondary and indirect to influence to their youth culture (e.g. guideline or behavior provided by popular movie actors or media figures) ; youth individuals culture can also

identify with a social class and the values of this class can influence youth behavior, e.g. school culture or working class. However, culture in its widest sense influences youth buying behavior and deference to suppliers can differ significantly between different countries' youth culture to choose to sell their products or provide their services to the countries' youth markets. Youth needs are also influenced by the situation in which youth currently find themselves in their countries. The subjects of age and socio-economic status can have profound effects on youth buying behavior at different youth age market segmentation, such as youth client groups can divided to any companies to concentrate on selling, e.g. between 20 ages to 40 ages or between 10 ages to 20 ages etc. different age groups.

In conclusion, marketer may learn more about youth culture from different countries' family life cycle stages of change which have sought to take account of their increasing complexity to influence to estimate the countries' youth buyer numbers. The family relationships can include single parent family, married parent family, no children family youth buyer groups of family life cycle youth buyer changing numbers in marketers' target countries. Due to all different countries family life cycle youth buyer numbers can indicate the countries' youth individual needs changing numbers and the target countries' youth buyer numbers are likely to change their purchase tastes and needs as youth culture goes through life. Hence, marketers can measure the target countries youth age segmentation estimate numbers to decide how many products or how much services to supply to them to satisfy their needs accurately.

CHAPTER FOUR

Salespeople client segmentation promotion strategy is England wine bar major successful factor

1. Critically evaluate the bases that bars may use to segment their markets.

The United Kingdom bars market is a mass marketing, it means a strategy that presumes these is one undifferentiated market and that the bars wine drinking service provision will appeal to all consumers in that similar bar market. Marketing matching strategy divides segmentation, it means act of dissecting the marketplace into submarkets (segments) that require different marketing mixes, then targeting, it is the process of reviewing market segments and deciding which one(s) to pursue finally positioning, it needs to establish a differentiating image for a product or service in relation to its competition. segmentation variables may divide geographic, demographic, psychographic and behavioral variables.

In general, marketers may use a single variable or two or more variables. Geographic segmentation is based on the location of the target market, people living in the same area have similar needs that differ from living in other areas, climate, population, taste and micromarketing. Demographic segmentation is based on factors, such as age, gender, marital status, income, occupation, education, ethnicity. Psychographic segmentation is based on lifestyle and personality characteristics. Behavioral segmentation is based on attitudes toward or reactions to a product/service and to its promotional appeals, usage rate, benefits sought from a product/ a service and loyalty to a brand or a store.

There are three basic market targeting strategies, such as undifferentiated, differentiated and concentration. Undifferentiated strategy ignores differences between groups within a market and offers a single market mix to the entire market and it works when a product/service is new to the market and there is minimal or no competition. Differentiated strategy means targeting two or more segments with different marketing mixes for each, concentration strategy focuses on one sub-market. Most British towns would had many small bars, all looking fairly similar to each other, with relatively few point of differentiation. Thus, if the UK bars do not use to segment their markets. I believe these UK bars will face much competition between themselves. In general, the market for drinking in pubs was fairly homogenous, comprising mostly male, who went to the pub mainly to drink and only very rarely to eat.

Now, UK pubs, clubs and bars continues to be a popular leisure activity in UK and pubs have benefits from a growth in eating out.

But, pub operators face challenges , including taxes on alcohol, growing competition from supermarkets for off sales, a smoking bad introduced. Pub operators have had to focus the design of bars on meeting the needs of smaller and smaller market segments. No longer is the pub market dominated by males going out to drink-professional women and families are among many segments and the professional and families segments, who seems dislike loud music or big screen television, who like to drink good quality coffee served more than beer, who like to enjoy bright and airy decorative in bars, who like to drink served to the table rather than queuing at the bar. These may have been design features that were unsought or unwanted by the traditional male heavy drinker segment. Hence, it seems that UK female professionals and families shall be the popular segment in this UK bars market. However, segmentation can not be based simply on where people live, and must recognize their mobility and movement patterns. Therefore, for some sites located in town centers or on busy roads, an understanding of people's work patterns and commuting habits can be crucial. Being near a train station may be crucial for attracting a target market or urban professionals who want somewhere to stop off to meet friends before catching a train home. I think the UK bars may use to segment their market. Segmentation is essentially about identifying groups of buyers within a marketplace who have needs that are distinctive in the way who deviate from the average consumer. Some consumers may treat satisfaction of one particular needs as a seek to satisfy any of needs from a car purchase total market, the possible factor that might influence and individual's choice of car, car market segment targeted includes status, safety for families, a particular image, a cost effective transport, seeking environment by buying a green car and a company buyer saves tax client groups. Hence, British bars are fairly similar to each other, with relatively few points of differentiation. The market for drinking in bars was fairly homogenous and British supermarkets can sell wines and the comprising mostly males who went to the bar mainly to drink and only very rarely to eat. Today, the bar scene in any British town centre is much complex. Hence, I think British bars ought to segment their markets if which wanted raise their competition.

On the first hand , the UK bar owner can choose professional women and family segment, in upmarket local, low density housing areas, it is likely to offer high quality food, no loud music or big screen television, good quality coffee served more than beer, bright and airy bar environment, drinks served to the table, rather than queuing at the bar, due to the proportion of women using these bars is higher than most of the locals.

On the second hand, the UK bar owner can choose male segment, in basic or mid market locals, that were unsought or unwanted by the traditional male areas; trade is focused on regular drinkers and tend to be met lead with little food. Beer, cider and spirits are the big sellers. Most show televised most offer some sort of food. There may also be themed evenings, quizzes, darts or pool. Customers tend to use the bar to meet friend and relax.

On the third hand, the bar can choose young local customers aged 18 to 30 secondary and university students segment. Amusements including pool tables and machines with feature and chart music and video screen will be prevalent.

On the fourth hand, the bar owner can choose city local to workers and shoppers segment, such as non office labors and supermarket buyers clients, it will offer basic bar food and snacks as well as centrally located in town centers but offering high levels of food, city dry led bars target the same customers as city locals, but focus on office labor clients mainly and it tends to be large and it may have function rooms and restaurant areas.

On the fifth hand, the bar owner can choose office workers and shoppers both segments. It may locate in centrally city location, but it needs to change from day to night to attract different types of customers. It can provide coffee bar attract in the day serving office workers and shoppers, but provide wine attract to young people's bar with loud music by might.

On the sixth hand, the bar owner can choose bar is located on or near the young non student people's circuit. Expect loud music, possibly a dress code and door staff and food is less important.

On the seventh hand, the bar owner can choose adults no children targets, in more upmarket areas. Restaurant quality food served for whose premium dining aim.

On the eight hand, the bar owner can choose family with children target, it again focuses on food these bar offers good value for money dining during the weekend and early evening.

On the final hand, the bar owner can choose to meet point for a specific customer group for example bikers, sport client segment in bicycle areas. It may be live music or entertainers to drink whose wine after who ride bicycle to need to find restaurant to sit down to relax and eat food needs. Hence, UK bar market is such as car sale market to follow family life cycle, gender and household composition, age, ethnic group, social class, individual income, lifestyles, individual attitudes, values benefits sought, the bar loyalty, the bar geographic location etc. the client internal psychological factors or the external environmental factors to divide different segments to sell in the market. However, I suggest the UK bars market segment ought to analyze to target young adult wine drinkers mainly. Bar consumer segmentation in the wine industry takes on many forms: demographic, geographic, behavioral and others.

For the bar wine industry, this group currently fits the legal drinking age range of 21 to 28 ages. With the recent oversupply of wine bars on the UK local market, so UK wine bars competitions are very high. Due to this situation, I recommend who need to focus efforts on finding new populations of wine existing consumers, rather than just redoubling efforts with existing clients.

I think wine bar marketers in the United Kingdom have primarily focused on the existing population of wine bar old consumers, which are the very large baby boomer young generation. This was an effective strategy for many years, when the wine supply and economic conditions were stable. Now, however, one of the most promising of the new wine bar consumer segments in the UK is that of the boomer generation. Generally viewed as children of the baby boomers. This segments group is considered whose consuming power and represented the future bars market for most wine brands drinking in UK bars. The children of the boomers who are young and who ought like to meet friends to go to bars to drink different kinds taste of wines and play entertainment in bars during who have school holidays. UK bars market segmentation means the process of dividing which different drinking wines taste into meaningful, relatively similar and identifiable segments or groups. In general, UK bars market segmentation is useful for two major reasons. First, it assists bars marketing searchers in analyzing the needs of a specific customer segment. Second, the resulting data, it allows bars marketing campaigns to be focused on these identifies needs. In the long run, this allows bars to spend their marketing and advertising budgets wisely when at the same time meeting the needs of the drinking wine customer. Ideally, this should result in efficient, effective and profitable bars marketing and sales efforts. There are multiple types and levels of segmentation used in various industries, but those used most frequently by the wine bar industry are those that also fall into for four classic marketing segmentation bases. There are geographic, which is based on where the customer lives, such as big cities or small cities, demographic, which is based on age, gender, income, social class, psychographic, which is based on lifestyle and personality and behavioral which is based on occasions, benefits, usage rate , readiness to purchase stage.

In bars business, the wine taste is main factor to influence the clients choose to come to the bar again. In general, there are five consumer segments, such as conservative, knowledgeable wine drinkers; image oriented, knowledge seeking wine drinkers, basic wine drinkers, experimental, highly knowledge wine drinkers and enjoyment oriented, social wine drinkers. Anyway, psychographic factor can influence people choose to go to bars, the psychographic wine segments identify five major wine lifestyle, such as relaxed lifestyle, dining ambience, fun and entertainment, social aspiration and travel lifestyle. Hence, psychographic factor and wine taste knowledge factor are reasons why people choose to go to bars to drink wines instead of who choose to go to supermarkets to buy wines to drink. Regarding geographic segments in the wine industry, it includes individual wine bars or organizational wine bars or supermarkets or stores wine sale methods in UK country. Regarding wine consumption behavior is another factor, it includes five segments: Super-core, who consume wine daily; core, who consume wine at least two or three times per month; marginal, who consume wine at least two or three times per quarter ; non adopters, who don't drink wine, but drink other alcoholic beverages and non drinkers who don't on the areas where are not close to supermarkets or stores and the living people who are super core to consume wine daily in the areas. The bar has more chance to increase client numbers, it is unconsidered whether the bar's wine taste can satisfy its clients needs. However, the young age market segment has very high consuming power. They don't only have a lot of money, but who influence family purchase. Many perform the grocery shopping for their families and have been given parent co-signed credit cards at a young age.

A key question in market segment analysis for this group is: What drives their purchasing behavior regarding wine? Young people can spend on average of 16.7 hours per week on the internet, excluding e-mail. They use it for shopping, in chat rooms, for research and to keep up is their primary source of information and who trust it. Because of this focus, wine bar marketers are urged to use integrated media to reach young people and not use only traditional channels. Online technology is a critical part of this,, but also offline locations where, such as music clubs, wine bars magazines, cable television and outdoor posters. E-mails targets at online interest groups and cell phone marketing are also useful. However, wine bars advertising that ought includes diversity of race and gender. In addition, young people are highly influenced by minority cultures in terms of music, sport, dress and language. The wine bars marketing implication is that advertising should show a variety of diversity in terms of race and gender. Another consideration is to emphasize values and focus on cultural values when targeting specific ethno-centric segments of young people population in UK. I believe why wine bars can attract more young people, it is due to their focus on wine brands and who like to attempt different new or old wine taste, young people are very wine brand conscious and seek wine brands that provide quality, but at a fair price. Anyway, young people market segment characteristics is their belief in fun and responsibility, who tend to believe that life should be fun and enjoyable, but at the same time who do want responsibility and challenge on the job, who want to make sure that who take time out to enjoy life and believe that certain activities, so I feel young people accept to drink wine in base , the possibility is more than old people or adult ages people.

In conclusion, I think this UK bar market is an undifferentiated mass marketing, due to any bars characteristics can only give places to provide similar tastes of wines or coffees drinking or foods and entertainment for clients to enjoy to single formulation of its food provided services, to bars have traditionally offer one standard of food service delivery to all of their domestic or foreign customers. Due to UK small, middle and large size bars and supermarkets and restaurants are increasing to cause competition seriously. Overtime, however, bar consumers‘ needs tend to fragment into segments of different needs. Where UK bar markets are competitive, a bar may no longer to able to ignore the bar clients whose special needs of small groups of its customers, because if bar owner sold similar taste of wines, coffees drinking and foods to its competitors of bars and restaurants and supermarkets, I believe the non segment bar will lose many clients to compare the segment bar in UK bar drinking wine restaurant industry.

2. In the context of bars, discuss the relative merits of quantitative and qualitative approaches to market segmentation.

In UK bars market, I think it had the relative merits of quantitative and qualitative approaches to bars market segmentation. As UK bars market segmentation, the UK bar owners need to identify groups of bar customers who have similar needs and respond in a similar way to a given marketing stimulus to raise their bar competition. Hence, UK bar owner may use segmentation to measure whether whose bar ought to choose to locate where location (areas) to provide which kinds taste of wines, coffees, foods and entertainment to attract which kind of bar client group mainly, e.g. if the bar target client group is professional office female, it can locate at upmarket location in low density housing areas. It is likely to offer high quality food because there are many professional office female clients are in these low density housing living. However, bars market segmentation should be regarded as the bar wines and coffees drinking and entertainment service provision of critical thinking rather than as some pre-determined set of procedures.

It shall follow that to let the bar owner to know what is an appropriate basis for the bar segment and one client group market may not be appropriate to all bar client groups in the UK bars market. To aware of the criteria by which the effectiveness of any UK bars segmentation basis can be assessed. I shall indicate those four important criteria to measure the relative merits of quantitative and qualitative approaches to UK bar market segmentation which can earn. The four important criteria include the usefulness to the UK bars marketing planning; the size of the resulting to the UK bar segment; the UK bar measurability and the UK bar accessibility four criteria. On the usefulness to the UK bar's marketing planning criteria hand, it needs to ask this question before which chooses who is whose bar target client group and location and wine and food taste. Is the basis of bar market segmentation useful to the bar owner? It is easy to develop bases for market segmentation when losing sight of the purpose of the exercise. Essentially, the exercise is worthwhile only bar segmentation allows the UK bar owner profitably to penetrate a greater proportion of UK bars market then would have been the UK bar market case if the exercise had not been undertaken. UK bar market client groups identified as homogeneous bar market segments must be just that: Similar in terms of the needs of tastes of wines or coffees drinking and entertainment consumption behavior of the domestic or foreign individual client who contain. The UK bar shall fail in whose segmentation exercise because its assumptions about homogeneity within a bar segment, e.g. male or female or young student or young non student or family with children or family without children or bicycle sport client or office of non office segment, who overlooks some critical differences within the bar segment which leads to varied responses to the bar service offering that has been specifically targeted at the bar client segment. For example, a bar segment for the office workers target client group, instead of the bar owner needs to consider the location whether it is located to close to whose office, who also needs to consider these factors such as, what kinds of foods , wines, coffees drink taste and what kind of entertainment and service price charge and their habit consumption time. To be more effective, bar market segmentation must recognize the diversity of needs within this bar target client group. Hence, the bar can measure to quantify and quality its bar target client group to produce its bar market planning effectively.

On the size of the resulting to the UK bar segment criteria hand, the UK bar owner ought need to ask this question: Are the segments of an economic size to whose bar business? Any basic for bar segmentation should yield segments that are of a size that the bar can profitably exploit, because as the bar segments

get smaller who get closer to achieving the marketing philosophy of satisfying each bar client's needs as though each one were the center of the bar's attention. The problem for the uneconomic to provide for what a reasonable size of bar segment is varies from one UK bar market to another and is constantly changing over time. In the bar market , it is possible to provide quite unique tastes of wines or foods to target very small segments of the UK bar market. For example, if the bar target client group is professional female office worker clients. I think it ought need to locate its bar in the office areas location and the office and the office can not be close to supermarkets because supermarkets will have different style of wines and coffees to sell and its provision of cup of wines and coffees drinking and foods tastes must be different to supermarkets wines and coffees and foods tastes and the bar needs to consider what the entertainment is the professional female worker clients who need to enjoy in the quiet or noise bar environment. Because this factors will influence the bar's female professional workers' psychological needs and satisfactory needs. If who feel the bar's drinking and food and entertainment service provision which can't satisfy whose demand, who can choose another bars to close to office areas to cause the bar female client numbers will reduce. On the UK bar measurability criteria hand, the UK bar owner needs to ask this question: Can the bar market segment be measured? Ideally UK bar should be able to know the precise size of its identified bar market segment(s).

This is imported in order that the bar segment(s) can be compared and its profit potentials assessed. Unfortunately, UK bars clients data are often not available to the UK bar quantity market segments. So the UK bar owner should believe the areas of bar clients exist but can't measure or the bar client numbers should define bar segments only on the basic of what it can accurately be measured, but the different areas (location) bar clients may have litter bearing on the homogeneity of bar consumers' needs and consumption aims or reasons. The UK bar market segments information have include, e.g. the age profile of an area, number of people per household etc. However, bar owner also needs to assess of individuals psychological subjectively factor, such as whose attitude and lifestyles, e.g. if the professional female worker who does not like to drink coffee or wine drinking, even the bar location is close to the professional female worker office client, it will not persuade who to enter the bar. Hence, the UK bar owner needs to find the areas where people whose lifestyles and attitudes to bar enjoyable feeling, then it may decide to measure whether the area (location) may have which bar target group(s) is/are the largest numbers to choose which kind taste of wines, coffees drinking and foods provision and which kind of entertainment to satisfy the bar's identified target client group(s) needs. Finally, on the UK bar accessibility criteria hand, the bar owner ought to ask this question: Are the segment(s) accessible to where bar business? There is little points to define the UK bar owner segment(s) of the UK bar market whose those bar segments are not accessible to the bar segments are not accessible to the bar owner or ever likely to be inaccessibility can come about for a number of reasons. Such as the UK bar owner may be prohibited by law from opening to locate whose bar in certain areas in UK geographic location (areas) or the UK law prohibits UK bar to sell some kind of taste of wines in whose country. Hence, the UK bar owner needs to know UK law prohibition to which kind of taste of wines drinking sold and where location (areas) to open its bars before who decides where to open its bar to sell wine to whose target clients segment(s) in British country. In conclusion, the UK bar owners can earn the relative merits of quantitative and qualitative approaches to market segmentation from these four criteria consideration.

CHAPTER FIVE

Supermarket salespeople training strategy is not Tesco supermarket major successful factor

1. Identify the elements of the value chain involved in the supply of fresh fruit and vegetables to Tesco stores.

The place(P) of the traditional marketing mix decides about channel intermediaries or middlemen to use an outdated, yet user friendly, term and the management of physical distribution. Placing products involves managing the process supporting the flow of goods or services from producers to consumers.

The process has sometimes been described as developing the best routes to market for a firm's products. Products must be made available in the right quantity, in the right location, and at the times when customers wish to purchase them. Marketing channels can perform an important role in the later stages of a value chain, in particular outbound logistic (e.g. order processing, storage and transportation); marketing and sales (e.g. market research, personal selling, sales promotion) and after sales service. However, it depends on which kinds of business to need outbound logistic, such as Tesco supermarket only needs ordering fresh fruit and vegetables from local farmers, then these foods need to be stored in refrigerate in warehouse and transport these foods to different supermarkets by vans. So, Tesco value chain only needs outbound logistic activity, but it does not need marketing and sales and after sale service to sell its fresh fruit and vegetables to its clients from its supermarkets (stores). In fact, Tesco stores

is such UK farmer's intermediaries which can add value by breaking bulk. This might involve purchasing in large quantities of fruits and vegetables from UK local farmers and then selling smaller, more manageable, to keep volumes of fresh food stock in warehouses, then its vans will deliver these fresh fruits and vegetables to different stores daily. Discrepancies of fruit foods quantity are reduced by Tesco (intermediary) who provides every store clients with individual preferable fresh foods items that suit their needs daily. Tesco stores can offer superior knowledge of a target market compared with farmers, for example by ensuring which kinds of vegetables or fruits foods numbers are stocked in every store to match the economic and lifestyle needs of Tesco store shoppers who live in the area. Probably the most important gaps between Tesco store shoppers and UK local farmers in channel management are indicated at those of location and time. A location gap occurs owing to the geographic separation of farmers and the store shoppers of their fresh fruit and vegetables foods. UK farmers generally want to grow their fruits and vegetable food in one central location (farming), but farmers‘ food buyers typically want to buy their growing foods locally. A time gap arises when the UK local farmers' fresh foods buyers want to buy whose fresh growing foods at a time when a UK local farmer may considerate it inconvenient to make the available. UK local farmers may like to grow fresh fruits and vegetable foods at night from 8:00 PM to 12:00PM, then who will collect these fresh foods
from 5:00 AM to 7:00 in the morning, but their buyers may want to buy in the evenings or at weekends afternoon. Tesco stores (intermediary) need to facilitate vans to transport these fresh fruits and vegetables foods from farmers‘ farming to its one central warehouse to deliver to different stores to sell the budget numbers of different kinds of foods to every local store consumers more exactly (Adrian, P. 2012).

Tesco stores is one of the world's largest retailers, it has social responsibility to protect fresh fruit and vegetable to sell to clients. It had attempted to predict customer behavior about hope much fresh fruit and vegetable and what kinds of fresh fruit and vegetable whose consumers will buy from data statistic in warehouse. It aims to reduce excess fruit and vegetable stocks in warehouse to cause perishable. In the winter might have seen choice reduced to basic items such as potatoes, cabbage, apples, supplemented by canned fruit and vegetables. Look in a Tesco supermarket today, and clients may find difficult to tell the season of the year or the distance from the countryside, simple based on the fruit and vegetables with are on display. In UK supermarket sector is intensely competitive, and has seen continuous innovation in the way it seeks to satisfy customers' needs. As consumers have become wealthier, the supermarkets realized that buyers would no longer be content with the staple foods such as cabbage and potatoes in the depths of winter-significant numbers of them now wanted excitement on a plate, and all year round. Furthermore, if they were planning a menu, they wanted to be sure that when they went to their local supermarket.

By and large, supermarkets have been key drivers of the value for the groceries that they sell. They have been close to their customers and identified their changing needs. They have built confidence with their customers, who can trust freshness and provenance of food they sell and the reliability of supply. It is therefore the supermarkets who have gone seeking sources of supply, rather than growers aggressively seeking to sell the produce that they have available. Before, the development of very large supermarket chains, retailers were more

fragmented. They did not have the power or resources to innovate with new product lines which they could then commission a grower to produce. Today, supermarket such as Tesco invest heavily in their food technology laboratories, and can then go to suppliers and place large orders with exacting standards with regard to price, quality, and delivery. Above all else, supermarkets have put themselves at the center of a slick distribution system which connects an international networks of growers through transport networks of trucks, ships and planes to put fresh produce in their network of stores, every day, all year around. The efficiency of the logistics, and the bargaining power of the supermarkets has often led to the price being charged at a British supermarket being lower than the price changed in supermarkets thousands of miles away where fruit and vegetables were grown. Tomatoes grown in Bulgaria and sold in Britain can be cheaper in Britain in local Bulgarian shops. The bizarre situation has occurred where the supermarkets import apples from France to be sold in Kent, the traditional home of British apple growing, plums from Poland to be sold in the grown product in Lincolnshire. Supermarkets argue that sourcing from overseas is not just an issue of cost saving more importantly, the supermarkets seek a continuity of supplies from large growers who can guarantee to deliver a specified quantity at a specified quantity at a specified time and place. The supermarkets capable of achieving this. British supermarkets are among the most efficient in the world, and their desire to ensure that customers can always get what they want may explain the mass transport of food. Local farmers‘ market may could environmentally friendly, but they rarely guarantee a continuity of supplies. As part of their drive for efficiency, supermarkets have a tendency to move food , such potatoes could being transported several hundred miles between distribution centers before they end up on a supermarket shelf just a few miles from where potatoes were grown. The environmental campaigning group Sustain has estimated that the average children travels 2,000 between the farm where it was grown and the supermarket shelf and furthermore the distance products travel from farm to end customer increased by an estimated 25 per cent between 1980 year and 2007 year (Priesnitz 2007).

Global warming had become an important issue with many clients and there was growing concern that supermarkets' practice of transporting fresh produce long distances around the world was irresponsibly adding to greenhouse gas emissions. Hence, distance travelled was one of value chain factor Terso supermarket needs to consider their fruit and vegetables food to keep fresh in refrigerate to transport to retailers to sell in UK. The most contentious food miles are clocked up by fresh fruit and vegetables flow in by plane from overseas. Although, air freighted produce accounted for less than 1 per cent of total UK food miles, it was the fastest growing way of moving foods around. One response By Tesco was to introduce a greatest proportion of local produce. To achieve this, it placed buyers and marketing teams in the regions in order to get a clear picture of local markets and to develop relationships with suppliers. By 2007 year, Tesco claimed to have 7,000 regional lines from throughout the UK, which were promoted as local produce, supporting local growers and reducing greenhouse gas emissions. Throughout its history, Tesco has demonstrated its ability to listen to what customers want, and this has been true in respect of its distribution system. The weaknesses of commodity systems are particularly for major customers, such as Mc Donalds, commodity systems do not lead to reliability in supply, quality, quantity or price nor high rates of innovation on which they can differentiate their offer from their competitors. The opportunity and challenge of fresh food product differentiation, so Tesco stores need to innovation to give rise to a number of strategic options to keep vegetables and fruits to be fresh in the short time to sell full numbers. If a firm, such as Tesco is the lowest cost producer than commodity market strategy can be an attractive strategic option. As Tesco stores fresh food sale that it's larger competitors shall find difficult to copy. Otherwise, Smaller size stores can sometimes be a competitive advantage.

Tesco stores (fresh food retailer) need to co-operate with suppliers and fresh food growers to align the whole chain to the changing needs of consumers. The food chain strategy aims to deliver superior value to specific groups of customers.

Tesco stores work closely with its fresh food suppliers to develop specific products for each range. Both the supplier and growers understand the Tesco marketing strategy and their role in the innovation process. Tesco is actively seeking new

chain ideas and is prepared to pay for such efforts. From a primary producer and supplier perspective the range of brands enables Tesco to work with suppliers to market the total crop .

2. Critically discuss the factors influencing Tesco's sourcing of fresh fruit and vegetables.

At a time when the media enjoyed the big supermarkets, such as Tesco, being seen to source fresh fruit and vegetables food locally and being good to the environment helped to restore. One observe from Friends of the Earth noted the local produce sold at a branch of Tesco in Excess had in fact travelled served hundred miles as it was moved from the grower to a regional processing center, then to a regional distribution center, and finally back to the supermarket where it was sold. There has also been debate about where sourcing fruit and vegetables locally actually reduces greenhouse gas emissions. There is an argument that Tesco supermarket would be better for environment to grow them in countries where fresh fruit and vegetables need less heating and fertilizers than if they were grown in British. The greenhouse gas emissions resulting from growing them locally in Britain may be more than the emissions associated with transporting them from warmer countries.

The first factor influences Tesco's sourcing of fresh fruit and vegetables is the main stages of horticultural value chain are as follows: The first stage is inputs elements needed for production, such as seed, fertilizers, agrochemicals fungicides and pesticides, farm equipment and irrigation equipment, production for export includes the production of fruit and vegetables and all processes related to the growth and harvesting of the produce, such as planting, weeding, spraying and picking, packaging and cold storage means grading, washing, trimming, chopping, mixing, packing and label are all processes that may occur in this packing stage of the value chain . Once the produce is ready for transport, it is chilled produce is ready for transport, it is chilled and placed in cold storage units ready for export, processes fruit and vegetables include dried, frozen, preserved, juices and pulps. May of these processed add value to the new foods by increasing the shelf life of the fruit and vegetables and the final stage is distribution and marketing means the produce is distributed to different channels, including supermarkets and small scale retailers and wholesalers and food services.

The second factor indicates several basic conditions must be for a country to enter the fresh fruit and vegetables value chain. These include climate allowing for year found supply, adequate road and transport infrastructure, such as ports and airports, essential for moving fragile foods to market efficiently, establishment of sanitary and to prevent disease spreading. The value chain needs to upgrading into the packing segment and processing segment. Upgrading into parking is dependent on understanding the market needs investment in capital goods and availability of supporting activities within the country, such as United Kingdom. Maintaining open lines of communication regarding demand preferences in fresh foods, quality, packing and fostering buyer involvement is critical in all stages of the value chain. For example, organize trips to key markets and they observe interactions at the point of fresh food purchase, a wide variety of equipment to attain very high standards of hygiene within the pack house operations as well as on site laboratories for fresh fruit and vegetables research and staff health tests, horticultural sector has been greatly inhibited in its upgrading along the value chain by the lack of fresh food quality packing materials. Much of produce destined for the Europe is shipped to neigh countries where it is repackaged, resulting in a significant of value. However, upgrading into the processing segment of the value chain has been difficult to achieve for low income developing countries since the processing of fruit and vegetables is cost prohibitive at low levels of crop production. Therefore, countries must gain a level of expertise during the production stage to increase output to a level that will enable the country to upgrade to the fruit and vegetable processing stage. For example, given the importance of ability to read pesticide labels and understand barcodes amongst others, standards have led to additional training initiatives to improve adult literacy. Skills training must be carried our in all job categories of value chain to maximize growth and upgrading opportunities. Investments in training are required for all job categories, from farm workers to managers, such as farming activities and the workforce within the agriculture sector, packing and storage positions and the processing stage in which workers are classified under the industrial workforce. Hence, fresh fruit and vegetables packing and processing services, such as washing, chopping, mixing as well as bagging, branding and applying bar codes are often carried out at the fresh foods source rather than at the end market destination. These processes which were previously based in the developed country, such as UK have created considerable new employment opportunities in developing countries.

The third factor influences Tesco's sourcing of fresh fruit and vegetables, which indicates today, the fruit and vegetables sector operators as a buyer driven value chain and large supermarket chains are the leading actors both in key export markets with controlling market and shares across the Europe and United States as well as increasing in emerging markets. These buyers including Sainsbry's Marks and Spencer and Walmart seek enhanced cost competitiveness, consistency and product differentiation, such as convenient, ready to eat fresh foods from their global supply chains. It causes considerable value chain method how fruit and vegetables are produced, harvested, transported, processed and stored to achieve how fresh fruit and vegetables characteristics of quality, size, pesticide use and the social and environment conditions of cultivation and post-harvest handling will influence buyer behavior decision. This ensures that the perishable food reaches its destination in good condition cold storage units are used throughout the chain to keep the produce fresh and both air and sea freighting supported by the cold chain are key elements to ensure timely delivery. Export is divided between production for fresh and vegetables and fruit consumption and production for processed fruit and vegetables that are not accepted for sale as fresh produce are as well as inputs for the processing stage, but in order cases, such as orange juice or preserved peaches a specific variety and grade quality is required and production occurs separately. The next segment is packaging and cold storage unacceptable low grade produce will be redirected to processing plants or the domestic market. Washing, trimming, chopping, mixing, packaging and labelling are other processes that may occur in this stage of the value chain. Once the produce is ready for transport it is chilled and placed in cold storage units ready for export. Packaging usually requires economies of scale due to the high costs of cold storage and other capital investment necessary at this stage .Processed fruit and vegetables include dried, frozen and preserved produce as well as juices. Processing plants purchase fruit and vegetables inputs from the producers. These firms may export their products under their own brands as well as under the buyer's brand. The last stage of the value chain before consumption is distribution and marketing. In this final stage, the produce is distributed to different channels including supermarkets, small scale retailers, wholesales and food services. Air freighting for horticultural foods and more cold storage segment of value chain in order to increase their access to key markets and avoid competition form new countries entering cold storage technologies allow suppliers to adapt to geographic constraints, such as size and distance to market.

3. Assess the level of power that Tesco exercises in the supply chain for fruit and vegetables.

The themes identified were the perceptions of freshness, having good relationships with growers and suppliers , good quality of fresh fruits and vegetables, competitive and pleasant environment for shoppers. Globalization of the fresh fruits and vegetables, retailer system has impacted on the distribution and marketing of fresh modern supply chain outlets now dominate the fresh food retail market. The increasing population and rising personal income is resulting in significant shifts in fresh food demand. Supermarkets are perceived to be the place where more wealthy consumers choose to shop. Consumers purchase almost everything there including fresh fruit and vegetable, meat, children and fish and other household supplier like dry food, bread, detergents, stationary and toys in supermarkets, such as Tesco stores, not choose to buy from fruit and vegetable markets or food retailers. The traditional markets and grocery stores comprise wet markets, fresh markets, farmer's markets are popular among consumers when purchasing fresh food are the oldest food distribution channel.

The traditional market has been defined as a market with little central control or organization that lacks refrigeration and doesn't process fresh foods into brands foods for sale where each vendor specialized in one fresh food line (meat, fish, fruit or vegetable) or in a sub line (fruit and vegetable). A fresh market and/or wet market generally occupies one or two floors of a building that is located adjacent to a housing area where there is a high population density and high traffic flow. The ground floor is normally rented to retailers who sell fresh food or ready to eat items. The upper live level is occupied by retailers who sell ready to items or non food products/ These stores are family owned retailers that sell a limited variety of foods ,such as fish, fruit and vegetable, bread and milk, stationary , toys and household supplies. However, consumers may limit their purchase from these stores due to the high prices and limited product lines. Another distribution power level to Tesco supply its fruits and vegetable to deliver to its clients in the short time. Tesco faces its customers occurred with respect to its home delivery service. With the launch of its Tesco online service, it effectively extended the supply chain right through to customers‘ own homes, adding value to its product offer by avoiding the need for customers to even visit a supermarket. Was it good for the environment to have fleets of delivery vans around town and countryside? Simple evaluations were difficult to make supermarket buyers again, Tesco was keen to be seen as a good citizen in this final leg of its chain, for example by launching electric delivery vehicles which Tesco decided to reduce global warmth when its vans do not need to deliver fresh foods and vegetables to different supermarkets from its warehouse in the long distance. Tesco stores is a retailer to UK local farmers that buys their fresh fruits and vegetable for the purpose of reselling them to end consumers in its different local stores daily. The Tesco stores are large, self service stores carrying a very wide range of different kinds fresh fruits and vegetable foods to sell in its different local value chains from UK local farmers supply daily. For example, Tesco stores are often the first with new store shoppers initiatives such as loyalty cards and low fresh food prices are based on large scale efficiency to sell in Tesco smaller independent stores to match. Hence, the factors can influence Tesco stores channel selection power include that the expectations of store shoppers who expect to buy local stores or who prepared to travel to a retailer that the farmers' fresh fruit and vegetables keep to save more than one day or more days to buy. This might mean taking into consideration factors such as a geographical preference to buy locally, or a tendency to feel more comfortable visiting a particular type of store; Tesco fresh foods attributes can be important, fresh produce that is highly perishable requires fairly short channels. Bypassing channels, a UK local farmer may seek to cut out intermediaries , such as Tesco stores by dealing directly with the public and Tesco may feel difficult to open up any new local stores for the farmers. Over saturation, a farmer may be accused of using too many fresh fruits and vegetable food distributors within a given geographical area, making it difficult for any individual distributor to achieve a satisfactory level of fresh foods sale , such as Terco stores. Too many links, in the supply fresh foods chain, Tesco stores may be required to buy excessive fresh fruits and vegetable foods from any farmers daily, who may be perceived as a fresh food farming competitor, rather than a cooperative channel member. New channels, these can have a similar effect to bypassing an intermediary, for example, many UK local farmers have opened up internet sales channels, thereby taking fresh food sales away from established intermediaries, such as Terso stores. Cost cutting, in order to increase volume fresh fruit and vegetables food sales, a UK local farmer may seek to distribute through higher volume, low cost intermediaries, which may make it more difficult for a smaller, full service intermediary , such as Terso stores sell the farmers' any fresh foods and UK local farmers can give incentives and rewards to other intermediaries to help them to sell in UK any stores to raise Terso's competition in UK foods supply market.

CHAPTER SIX

Salespeople training strategy is not major factor to hospital service industry

1. What do you understand by the concept of a pricing model? Critically discuss their relevance to a public sector service ,such as the England NHS public hospital.

A price model reflects the fact that companies can generate revenue through a variety of combination of the basic price and prices charged for optional additional items. Some price models may be sustainable by giving away a product at very low price initially, but then charge higher prices for essential items that are needed to make the product function. Sometimes, the dominant pricing model in a market is challenged by a new entrant, with the result that consumers' expectations are changed. The price model can occur in perfectly competitive market or non perfectly competitive market. A perfectly competitive market characteristics include there are many producers supplying the market, each with similar cost structures and each producing an identical product. No single supplier on its own influence the market price because it is not monopoly, water and electricity is managed by government to control the public utility company which can not charge high fee to every householder user at the reasonable price ; both buyers and sellers are free to enter or leave the market and there are no barriers to entry or exit and there is a ready of information for buyers and sellers, for example about competing alternatives, e.g. oil products and stock markets where shares are bought and sold are exist in perfectly competitive market. In perfectly competitive markets, firms are price taker and their ability to set prices is limited by the level of demand and supply within the market they serve. If the total demand go up, all other things being equal, the going rate of prices in the market for their product will rise. Likewise, if there is a drop in total supply for whatever reason (e.g. because of bad weather, there will be further pressure for prices in the market to rise. The final price paid in the market will reflect the balance between supply side and demand side factors.

The model of perfect competition presented the forces of competition may be ideal for consumers because the tendency of market forces to minimize prices and/or maximize firms' outputs. But in such markets, suppliers are forced to be price takers rather than price makers. in a perfectly competitive market, firms are unable to use marketing strategies to affect the price at which they sell. At a higher price, buyers will immediately substitute identical products from other suppliers. Lower prices would be unsustainable in an industry where all firms had similar cost structures. Otherwise, an non perfectly competitive market, firms are able to use marketing strategies to affect the price at which they sell. Such as UK medical service market , private hospitals and public hospitals and clinics which can raise their service fee to their patients to follow their patients demand due to their doctors and nurses service performance, medicines quality and price and patient beds supplies factors to influence their service charges to their patients in UK. Hence, NHS needs to provide different and excellent medical service to its patients to make them to feel it's service is better to other private hospitals and clinics if it wanted to apply price model to its car parking or hospital phone system service charge to its patients because it is a public sector medical service organization. It ought not charge extra service fee to its patients in its hospitals. If it charged extra service fee, such as car parking and hospital phone system service which are same or higher or lower than other private hospitals or clinic , which need to ensure which medicine quality, doctors and nurses performance which are better than private hospitals and clinics and its patient beds need have enough supply to any patients when who feel need to sleep in its hospital. Because NHS image is a non profit medical organization to any UK poor patients, who choose NHS medical service are due to its medical service charge is cheaper than private hospitals and clinics and who feel it can provide free car parking and free hospital phone system service.

A market is defined here need not be a physical location where exchange takes place (as happens in retail and wholesale grocery markets). A market in the economist's sense refers to all individuals and firms who wish either to buy or sell a specific product. A market is defined in terms of products or service and geographic description, so the UK soft drinks market refers to all individuals in the UK who seek to buy soft drinks and the suppliers to that market. The UK medical service market structure can describe as the number of consumers, such as patients and medical providers , such as private hospitals and public hospital , such as NHS (National health service) and clinics; the barriers that exist to prevent new private hospitals or clinics or public assistance hospitals from entering the UK medical service market (or prevent UK patients do not prefer to choose NHS medical service); the extent to which the supply medical services is concentrated in the UK small number patients normally and the degree of collusion that occurs between patients and/or private or public hospitals or clinics medical service providers in the UK medical market. Governments often seek to regulate the prices of key products and service, such as electricity and telephones and public hospitals medical services, so it is important to understand how firms can reconcile the sometimes conflicting approaches of market forces and regulation, such as NHS public sector medical service in United Kingdom. Of course, if NHS public sector medical service planned to charge some non major service fees, such as car parking and hospital phone calling service to its patients and hospital visitors and staffs which are same to private hospitals, it needs to consider pricing model should never be seen as an isolated element of hospital's marketing decision making. It needed to consider its service performance of its doctors and nurses, its social responsibility of public medical service image whether it is better or worse than private hospitals that it had created and NHS 's distribution strategy whether it's patient beds supply numbers are enough to patients and whether it's medicine quality and supplies and prices which are reasonable to compare to private hospitals or clinics in this medical service market in United Kingdom. Private business organization with a broad range if products or services are often price different with their portfolio in quite different ways. They may have developed a price model, which describes the way that it uses pricing of its portfolio to maximize its overall revenue. Hence, one product or service may be charged at a very low price, on the assumption that it can raise higher price if many clients choose to buy its product or consume its service. In some sectors, a number of different pricing models co-exist. For example, in the emerging multi-channel television broadcasting market, some channels are provided free of charge to users, but make revenue from selling advertising space, when others charge to users, either on a monthly/annual basis or a pay to view basis. The idea of a pricing model is familiar to private sector organizations, but do they have a role to play in the public sector? In the UK, pricing models are increasingly being discussed and developed for services which have previously been considered a vital service and available freely to all.

Adrian, P.(2012) showed that the National Health Service (NHS) has a long and proud tradition of providing health service to all, according to an individual's need, paid for out of general taxation, according to individuals' means. Pricing has historically had very little role to play in the NHS. However, from the mid-1990 year, individual NHS trusts began exploiting charges for ancillary services as a means of boosting their revenue. One of the first targets for charging was users of hospitals' car parks. Trusts argued that providing car parks was not central to the mission of NHS trusts, and conveniently, government was encouraging more people to use public transport and leave their cars at home. Critics argued that patients were essentially captive and public transport was not a realistic alternative for most people. However, it showed that at one hospital in London, a patient who attended A&E on the advice of her GP, was charged UK$3.75 for the first two hours' use of the hospital car park and UK$7.5 thereafter. She was ten minutes over the two hour period and therefore had to pay higher charge. She also questioned the fact that charges were reduced to UK$1 per hour after 6:00 PM, when many hospital departments were closed. For private sector service, a lower evening price, when there is not much demand from customers, and plenty of spare capacity, it quite common. But is it right that a hospital should only charges lower prices at the not busy time when much of the hospital itself is closed? If lower prices are designed to stimulate additional demand, it this a realistic prospect when many hospital departments are only available between 9:00 AM to 5:00 PM? Another source of revenue exploited by many hospital trusts from the use of bedside telephones by patients. Many trusts entered agreements with private telephone service providers which allowed incoming and outgoing patient calls only through the officially appointed system, which used a premium rate number. A proportion of the revenue was retained by the hospital. Conveniently, hospital trusts pointed to evidence that mobile phones could harm sensitive medical equipment , and therefore used this to eliminate competitive pressure from patients' mobile phones, forcing them to use the hospital's own telephone system. The ethic of hospital telephone pricing was challenged by the House of Commons Health Select Committee, which accused some trusts of using excessively outgoing call, adding to patients' costs, and boosting hospital revenue. It cited a hospital in Essex where people wishing to telephone patients were being charges 49p per minute at peak time and 39p off peak. By comparison , a typical household rate for a long distance phone call was around 7p in the peak and 2p in the off peak. The select committee also expressed doubts about whether a ban on mobile phones in hospitals was actually a result of possible interference with medical equipment and recommend visitors should be able to use mobile phone within certain areas of hospitals. So, it seems that UK private hospitals patients phone calling service fee is below than householder phone calling service fee and it is not every patient must need to use phone when who stays in hospital as well as the visitors should able to use mobile phones and who should not use hospital phones within certain areas of hospital, who will not interference with medial equipment. Otherwise, by banning mobile phones, had private hospitals been more concerned about creating a monopoly environment for pricing their telephone service, than any possible risk to their equipment? However, I think National health service (NHS) which is one public government assistant hospital, it can not be same to private hospital to charge unreasonable car parking fee or hospital phone service fee to its patients, due to these ancillary services is not hospital main income source and it is one non profit hospital, it needs to provide the fair and non expensive medial charges to its poor patient segment because who are not rich, so who will prefer to choose NHS medical service to compare to choose private hospital services in United Kingdom.

National health service (NHS) is a privatization, fragmentation and market competition of health care provision supposedly to cut costs and improve the efficiency of the health service in England. The NHS was set up in 1948 year to be a free and accessible care, publicly owned and funded sector service in England. NHS needs to consider to redefine its relationship with health service, limiting the quality and quantity of care it can expect to receive, how it access that care, who is delivering if and even how it is paid for. The result will be poorer, fragmented services with larger differences in quality and access. Services/treatments will cost more and the public will increasingly have to pay for aspects of its care that used to be free at the time of treatment. Traditionally privatization has been through the sale of public assets and services to private owners through the mass sale of shares, e.g. the sale of telecoms, railways, energy or water services. These companies than own the services and are able to make profits from them like any other are able private businesses. In the NHS until now, this model of privatization is taking place through a combination of the reduction of the role of government in regulating health provision, the transfer of services to the private sector through commissioning from any qualified providers, such as independent sector treatment care centers, outsourcing of parts of services to the private sector, the creation of market mechanisms for the distribution of funding within the NHS (e.g. commissioning, payment by results mechanisms, the purchaser-provider split and so called patient choice policies). The use of private finance initiatives that use private money to build new buildings and infrastructure and then the state has to pay, the creation of foundation trusts that are run much more like private businesses and have the ability to raise funding through private patients that pay for services, allowing services to become not for profit organizations, such as social enterprises, cooperatives or mutual and thus leave public ownership, limiting access to certain services previously provided by the NHS. Provided healthcare tends to cost more. It requires a large bureaucracy to operate, with huge transaction costs that come with contracts, billing and litigation. In general, as the proportion of private spending on health care rises, so does the overall cost. The creation of healthcare market can also impact upon the continuity of care people receive. There is always the threat that the private sectors or other providers who take on a service that doesn't secure the expected financial returns may cut losses and withdraw from the provision of that service. NHS is under increasing financial pressure. For example, surgery like hip and knee replacements are more expensive areas of care, the results cause the loss of training opportunities for junior doctors expenditure spending and other health professionals as ever large shares of routine surgery and medical procedures are diverted away from the NHS. Centers for research and medical innovations are also threatened. This can lead to service being out. NHS hospitals will therefore fail financially and be pushed into greater debt. This could lead to hospital mergers, closure or the private sector coming in to run the service on profit making contracts. NHS will bring poor health care service if it will not increase its service charge price to patients. The poor service will be caused, such as permanent damage may have been inflicted on patients with serious conditions due to the lack of follow up care after treatments. In a second worrying example dangerous delays affected the patients of a privatized out of hours. A competitive market system leads to greater rationing and gradually drives patients to take on more responsibility for funding their own care. It seems this already in the privatization of long term care and dentistry. Patients may soon have to top up the cost of their hospital care in the same way that many already do for community health services. The concern is that the NHS will provide a less comprehensive range of treatments. For the private sector, the aim is to make a profit from every contracts, which is not the same as providing the best service . For example, Southern Cross, where the need to make profit lead to the rapid closure of care homes, leaving old people with no home. Hospital people with learning disabilities and challenging behavior were subject to physical and psychological abuse. Privatization will lead to fragmentation of the health services. This is a process on a commercial footing and redesigning the system along market lives. With different organizations delivering different service in different locations, it is also likely to lead a new health service with some area receiving much better care than others, hardest, leading to greater health inequalities. Fragmentation of services leads to worse clinical outcomes as staff have less opportunity to work in a fully integrated dynamic multi disciplinary team. Patients with complex needs can be particularly considerable. The impact of privatization on current NHS staff, who are transferred from NHS employment to non NHS organizations would be changed terms and conditions at the time of transfer. These terms and conditions could be changes at some time in the future, staff would no longer be covered by the national negotiating arrangement in the NHS, meaning they would not be entitled to any future pay uplifts or agreed charges to the change terms and conditions of service . If staff moved from this employer to another outsourced community service, who would lose their entitlement to access the NHS pension scheme and would be treated as new staff rather then former NHS staff, the new service provider could argue that the service who will be providing is so different that they will not be requiring staff to transfer. Those staff will than be made redundant. In conclusion, NHS is one public medical service non profit organization. It's pricing model ought be public service price model, such as no price discrimination and non competitor based pricing aim. It may be difficult or undesirable to implement a straightforward price-value relationship with individual of public services for a number of reasons: Such as NHS public sector medical service pricing can be actively used as a means of social policy, subsidized prices are often used to favor particular patient segment groups, such as car parking fee charges to visitors or hospital staffs only as well as hospital phone system service charges to visitors only or prescription medical service charges favor the very ill and unemployed patients and low income patients and students patients.

2. What factors should influence the level of charges at an NHS car park?

Principles for fair hospital car parking, such as NHS is important because its car park service represents the hospital reputation. Charging for car parking is often necessary, but needs to be fair, providing a travel plan for users of all types of transport, controlling parking fairly, with concession for those whose health conditions or work commitments mean they have to park frequently or at anti social hours, showing car park and transport costs and how charges are invested, thinking about the environment and how transport can reduce the NHS 's impact , being open and involve patients and the public. It is important to get car parking and transport policy and it is

communication, right to ensure fair access, good patient and staff experience and to protect hospital organization , such as NHS reputation. Clinical and social changes as car ownership to patients, staff and visitors to hospital sites has increased. For services with rural or urban , as public transport infrastructure is less convenient and reliable . When for specialist treatment, some patients need to travel greater distance and modern hospitals have often been located on the edge of population centres.

Car parking is also a factor in patient's experience of using healthcare. When much progress has been achieves to improve the patient environment inside the hospital, including cleanliness and new buildings, patients frequently report dissatisfaction with transport and parking arrangement. Visitors concerns both cost of car parking and also the availability of space for people with an essential need, illustrating the competing demands that managers need to balance. Patient experience is an important objective for hospitals; poor experiences can undermine confidence in clinical quality and stress can be worsened by poor transport and parking policies. Car parking can have a major impact on the local and national reputation of the NHS hospital . As patient choice increases, reputation and loyalty will be key drivers for provider's commercial sustainability. It seems car parking is one important factor to influence patients who choose hospital more than location/ transport/ easy to get to/ reputation of consultants factors. Ensuring that patients can access hospital when they need to is an important part of healthcare delivery.

Many patients who need to travel to hospital by car, either because of mobility or illness, a lock of alternatives or through choice. However, providing a car park is not the only component of a travel plan. Access to healthcare should be considered in terms of service planning, decisions on location of services, building design, access routes and the other transport modes. One of the factor of the current changes to the way that NHS hospital services are delivered is that healthcare should be localized where possible. In many cases, people who used to have to travel to hospital are being treated in community health centers. The NHS hospital can also ensure services are accessible. Most notably, ease of access has recently been improved by reducing waiting times and by enabling patients to choose and book their appointment at a time and location that is convenient to them. Another of factor is whether NHS hospital had or had not ran a bus service from a nearby park and ride car park that runs every 15 minutes. The service has proved popular and is now run by the UK country council. The hospital is been to extend the shuttle service to the other three park and ride car parks which serve the city. The other factor influences NHS hospital charge includes the control parking fairly with concessions for those whose health conditions or work
commitments mean they have to park frequently or at anti-social ours. In order to ensure that those patients who really need to access hospital by car are able to NHS often need to ensure that car parking space is available on site. Space is usually constrained, NHS hospital is in city or town center with high land costs and planning constraints. Charging some patients, visitors and staff to park can manage demand for space when ensuring that those who really need to park are able to access services. Where charging is required to manage demand, the overriding principle should be to ensure that where possible those patients who have the greatest need to park are prioritized. Where managing demand is a reason for charging for car parking, there may be scope for varying rates for different times of the day and the week, for example, increasing charges for non essential users in peak hours but applying a minimal charge at night when there is less reason to ration space. As well as prioritizing car access for those with greatest needs restrictions on car parking may also be required to deter non hospital traffic, particularly where NHS hospital is located in controlled parking zones, near shopping centers or other facilities that might need to illegitimate required use of NHS hospital grounds. In these cases , NHS hospital may be required to be charge the same as local car

parks to avoid abuse by non visitors. However, alternative arrangement could also be explored, including day permits for people with appointment. NHS car parking fair policies should need to be fair application. This is often a cause of concern for patients and visitors. Concessionary schemes and season tickets should be well publicized and available, since a patient may not known in advance low frequently who will need to attend a clinic in the next month. Penalty charges, or towing away should only be applied extreme circumstances with a presumption of good faith that no patient or visitor chooses to stay in hospital longer than necessary and may how on arrival how long who will have to wait for treatment. Running a car park can be expensive. These are maintenance, security,
insurance and running costs and the NHS hospital has to pay for
the space the car park uses. Costs are particularly high where land prices are high or there is increased risk of crime. At the same time, patients and the public rightly don't expect healthcare to suffer to pay for parking. The transport costs of non car owners are not subsidized by the NHS budgets to provide subsidized free car parks . To make car parking fee would be to penalize those using public transport. Therefore, fair charging is often the most sensible answer to adopt these two demands. Climate charge and pollution and congestion factor also have health impacts. Reducing car dependency is also a public health objective in order to reduce traffic accidents and increase physical activity.

These NHS organizations have a number of environmental and health reasons to seek to encourage people to use other modes of transport. Parking charge together with the expansion of alternative bus an cycling options to encourage a modal shift from cars to alternative transport. Patients , visitors and staff need to be made aware of these aims. NHS hospital can achieve a travel plan to develop to its car parking with the aim of during a period of busy time reducing single occupancy car journeys by 15% over three years, ensuring tat patients and visitors do not have to search for a space for more than ten minutes at peak times, encouraging the number of direct bus routes to the site to increase reducing staff parking spaces per employee by 10% as staff numbers grow. Car parking charges were introduced as part of the plan with certain categories of staff on exempted from charges (night and weekend staff, disabled staff, volunteers, car sharers and tenants of residential accommodation. From an environmental perspective, NHS travel plan supposed to reduce numbers of cars arriving at the site and the numbers of bus car raise. It aims to improve bus services to cause air pollution at the busy car parking period and cycle parking spaces and improved cycle facilities have encouraged staff to commute by bike. Additionally, a park and ride scheme aims to reduce car traffic of the NHS hospital in the busy time.

Moreover, it is absolutely wrong to charge cancer patients regardless of income, for unavoidable parking costs. From a staff point of view, NHS hospital car parking is an indirect tax on healthcare. However, most unions also support the aim of reducing car usage, as long as policies are fair. Because NHS hospital needs to develop transport policies for patients requiring regular cancer treatment. This approach has potentially negative publicity into a positive image to public. These ought be free parking for the duration of a cancer patient treatment or as often as is needed.

Reference

Adrian, P. (2012). Introduction to marketing theory & practice,
3 rd edition, London: Oxford press.

Couper, M.P. J. Blair and T. Triplet (1999). A Comparison Of Mail And E-mail For a Survey Of Employees In USA Statistical Agencies. Journal Of Official Statistics, 15, 39-56.

Data monitor (2008). The proctor and gamble company. Retrieved Nov. 15 2009 from http://www.datamonitor.com/

Dyer, D., F. Dalzell & R. Olegario (2004). Rising tide. Lessons learned from 165 years of brand building at Procter and Gamble. Boston, MA: Havard Business School Press.

Priesnitz, W. (2007) Counting Our Food Miles. Natural Life, 1 July.

Sullivan, Nicholas P(2007). You can hear me now: How Micro loans and cell phones are connecting the world, San Francisco, CA: John Wilsey & Sans, 2007.

CHAPTER SEVEN

Customer unspoken experience factor influences business success

Can customer purchase experience influence business success? In general, we argue that the ability to achieve business success by focusing on the physical aspects of the product, e.g. quality, price or the delivery. We are less considering the feeling aspects of our customer purchase experience. Many businessmen do not understand salespeoples‘ sale behavior can influence any customer how to feel the brand's products image. Why can influence customer experience bring any business success. Generally, in consumption market, customers have similar products, similr salespeople, similar technology and similar pricing to choose to buy any kinds of products. Hence, how to influence customer experience, will let the customer feels good or bad image to the company as well as repeating purchase choice to the company's products again.

Customer expertise means the customer emotion whether he feels good or bad to the brand's product quality, reliability, pricing. It is not just about the company's salespeople services, it is about sales, marketing, web site design, systems, processes and overall staffs performances. Customer experience is differentiating solely on the traditional psysical elements, such as price, delivery, and lead times is no longer a business strategy. The customer experience is that differentiation. What is the best customer experience, e.g. in a shop, on a vacation, at a restaurant, on a flight? Any of these different consumption environment, which will influence any customer feels different consumption experience. However bad customer experiences are easy to produce.

A great customer experience can excit good customers' emotion. There are two elements to a consumer experience: The physical and the emotion. We are all human beings : Emotions are constant. They are there all the time. I believe that emotion side of the customer experience is the essence of first direct to compare the price of a product, its quality, the lead times for delivery. For a customer to put eh phone down, or click off the internet and not only know that something has been sorted, but feel good about it. These environment factors can influence the customer's purchase emotion will have long or short time of good or bad feeling to the product, e.g. within a week or two, the food is consumed and that experience has gone. For a car company, the consumer is living with his brand for up to three or four years following the day he bought the car. So, long or short customer emotion time, it depends on whether the product can be used how long. For restaurant example, when the restaurant's competitors can raise similar taste of foods, similar price, similar restaurant environment, e.g. size, location, design.

The competitive factor will be emotion factor, how to let its food customers feel satisfactory and comfortable and kindly waiters' serving feeling in order to bring short time good (positive) or bad (negative) emotion feeling after every had eatten all foods and prepare to pay money, till to leave the restaurant's whole eatting consumption time. So, it seems that emotion factor can influence whether food customers will repeat choose the restaurant to eat again. If the restaurant can let many customers to build short time good emotion feeling when they choose this restaurant won't loss many old food customers easily. Even they willl help it to persuade their friends to choose this restaurant to eat. Hence, customer serving experience will be one important factor to influence this restaurant's success, when it has many similar food taste, similar price, similar restaurant environment design and locations' competitors existence.

For product sale industry example, in general, manufacturers will focus on physical experience, e.g. price, availability, accessibility, efficiency , ease of use, range and delivery. They feel emotion experience is not important. For this suitation example, when one client had bought one computer from the computer shop. He brings it to home to use. Suddenly, we feel that this computer has some engineering functions, he does not know how to use, but he had left this computer ship to enquire its salespeople. If this shop company has one enquiry department, its staffs can answer any technical issues concern how to use this company's any function, due to any buyers can phone telephone hotline and it takes time to establish a call centre operation to let them to enquire , any computer function technical problem in order to any computer function technical problem in order to ensure their any problems correctly. Then they will have more food emotion, due to this company shop can improve its customer satisfaction for any technical problems in order to get solutions immediately from its call centre computer technician assistance service. Hence, this computer shop's sale after service will be one important factor to bring good customer purchase experience.

In general, the physical customer experience for either service provision or purchase business stages will follow as below:

Step one: The customer expectation to the product or service is setted by advertising, brand image, personal relation, word of mouth.

Step two: The consumer will make pre-purchase interacton, either quotes or information gathering.

Step three: When the consumer has choose to buy which brand of product or consume whom service provider, he will make purcahse interaction, ordering, activities and final purchase implementation.

Step four: After the consumer pays money to buy the product or consume the service, he will make evaluation, to using and consuming the product/service, it is post purchase interaction.

Step five: Post-experience review, it is intuitive review, customer experience and revise experience and expectation. It is the most important factor to influence the customer's emotion whether his feeling is good or bad after he used the product or consume the service. It is one most important customer experience final stage. Because this stage will influence whether the customer will choose to repeat to buy the shop's products to use again or consume the shop's service again.

During this restaurant's final customer experience stages, its physical and emotion both expectations will influence whether you , such as this restaurant food cusomer will be influenced to choose to eat its food again in the short time by your good emotion influence. I shall indicate this situations: In you order your food stage, the restaurant can provide the choise is adequate physical expectation and the server engages you in a discussion and is excited by the meal choice to your emotion expectation. In you need wait for your food to arrival stage, it can provide approprite length of the phsical expectation and it's sufficient time not to feel rushed in your emotion expectation. In your food arrival stage, you feel that it is the food you ordered and it looks appetising physical expectation and the server is smiling in your emotion expectations. In your eating food stage, you feel it is the correct temperature physical expectation and the sensations are pleasant in your emotional expectation. In your asking for your bill stage, you feel this is not as important as serving other customers physical expectation and the server smiles and hurries to get the bill emotional expectation. In your bill arrival stage, it takes an appropriate amount of time to time physical expectation and you expect it to be value foe money emotion expectation. In your leaving the restaurant stage, it provides you are thanked for coming physical expectation and you can also feel that you have a warm feeling they linked you being there emotion expectation. Finally, in your walking back to your can final stage, you feel that it doesn't cause you feel inconvenience or needing to pay extra car park fee, due to your choice to eating this restaurant's good, when you feel car park is still well to your physical expectation and you feel safe in your emotion expectation.

So, all of your food consumption in this restaurant's all stages can build good physical and emotional expectatons to satisfy your great customer experiences, during your short time eating process in this restaurant. Hence, this restaurant will let you feel good emotion, due to your hope can be met and exceed you positive expectations from this restaurant's service, exceed its negative service expectations and it can identify opportunities to exceed your mininal level physical expectations and emotion expectations to this restaurant.

On conclusion, nowadays customer experience factor will be more important to compare other factors to influence any businesses success. Due to customer individual good or bad emotion will be influenced by his/her post-purchase experience influence. Businessmen can not neglect how to satisfy their customers' past- good purchase experience feeling and building good emotion. It will be one important successful factor to compare other physical factors.

CHAPTER EIGHT

Is training an important factor to influence organization growth success

In any organizations, they must need salespeople to help them to sell products. Is any organizations' profit growth objective influenced by salespeoples' sales skills? Must salespeoples' training be the most important critical path to influence organizations' success? Must The organization growth be not successful, if the organization lacked enough
salespeople to help it to sell products? Have other factors more important than salsespeople skill to influence any organizations' growth in success? Can the organization still develop in success, if it has no enough salespeople to help it
to sell products? Otherwise, whether the organization can still succeed if it has other departments to help it to develop its
organization, e.g. human resource department, strategy department, marketing department, product development department? Is only
salespeople the critical path to influence any organizations' successes? I shall indicate organization's different departments' internal operation to explain whether salespeople number and skill is the critical or important path to influence any organizations' successes as below:

Is training salespeopls' skill goal to be prior to compare other goals in any organizations because every organization must need
salespeople to help them to introduce their products to let their customers to know in order to achieve sale easily. However, investing time to
train salespeople to raise their sale skills, must it help any organizations succeed to raise sale growth? I feel that any organizations'
intellectual sale growth ought not only concentrate om how to provide

training or improvement of salespeople skills. If the organization only concentrate on providing any kinds of training or improving its salespeople sale skill methods. It won't achieve intellectual sale growth easire
, even it must not achieve intellectual sale growh in possible success. I shall explain reasons to explain what the cause and effect relationship
is as below:

If the organization only concentrate on providing training or improving its sales skills to achieve its salespeoples' sale growth aim or
goals in either short term or middle term or long term. It will neglect to consider whether what other deparments' actual problems, they are facing. Their facing problems may include: Is its present marketing department's marketing strategy adapted to satisfy its customers' needs? Does it
need to review its present marketing strategy in order to change its weaknesses to be strengthes? Does its organizational management structure need tobe revised? Does its operational team memebers need to be changed other new one to replace its old operational team members, e.g. CEO, upper management members? Does its human resource department need to be changed its recruitment strategy, interview skills, interview method etc. different operational problem issues? So, if the organization only concentrate on how to provide training or raise or improve its salespeople sale skills. I believe that this organization won't achieve intellectual sale growth goals in success. Because one effective and efficient organization, it must need different departments co-operate to work together closely, in order to achieve productivity growth, efficiency growth, even sale growh goals.

Every department needs to concern how to achieve short term goals in priority, then they will achieve middle term goals, even long term goals
easily consequently. Thus, if one organization can not achieve or improve its any department itself short term goals in success. Then, its factory deparment workers or staffs can not be improved either its efficiency to be raised or shorten time to be reduced to manufacture its products or its human resource deparmtnet has not revised its recruitment strategy or interview method whether it needs in order to employ the most right staffs to do any positions in its organization. Then, its employees turnover number will be raised in possible when they feel work pressure or workload, or bringing negative emotion feeling
to excit their leaving organization desire. If these departments' staffs' performances are worse, then even their organization can provide enough

training
to improve their sales skills. It salespeople still can not influence their organization has sudden sale growth to guarantee success easily because this organization can not only depend its salespeople sale skill to be improved in order to help it to raise its products sale numerb growth. It must depend on different departments' close cooperation relationship together in order to implement final sales path success more easily consequently.
If the organization can not solve any departments' problems, then even it has good saleskillful salespeople to help it to sell its products, it won't still raise its sale growth more success in possible. Hence, solving all different departments' problems, this issue is prior important to compare to provide training to raise its salespeople' sales skill issue.

Does organizations need to implement how to plan and manage time control to their salespeople in order to achieve sale growth goal easier? Planning and time control is one critical path factor to improve salespeoples' sale skills method. Because when every salesperosn can have good self-discipline to control and manage
himself/herself personal behavior in his /her private time daily. Then, if he/she had good living habit, it can influence his/her sale performance or sale behavior to be improved consequently. Because salespeople have human nature, they will feel tried or lazy and their negative emotion may bring indirect relationship to influence
their sale performance to be worse in their working time. So, sales management ought need to teach them to learn how to arrange or manage their time between working time and private living time in order to adapt to their sales working environment more easily.

Hence, learning how to plan and manage salespeoples' time between working time and private time issue, it is more prior important to compare to provide training or sales skills to them. Because offence is that part of the salesperson's work in which he must take the entire consideration. It is one offense and defense concept. For example, defence, colored red , covers these activities which are forced upon salespeople by virtue of the way they make their living. As salespeople grow in the
process to spend every how to every day in service and related activities. If they attempt to do, they may help businessmen to earn the reputation of being the best service ro their customers. A salesperson himself/herself ability to grow as a talent or perfect salesperson, will someday the governed by his/her ability to control the defensive

demands on his/her time. These include his/her sale responsibilities to his/her employer demand and her/her industry , as well as regular paperwork during he/she spends time to work in his/her organization.

However, organizations alsoe need to spend time to educate salespeople to learn sale skills. The process begins with self education. In studying every prospective sales situation, a salesperson would first put himself/herself in the prospect's position. Then, he/she would analyze, every phaze of the problem and come to an objective conclusion about what he/she would doif he/she were the prospect. However, this part of the process is relatively easy and in varying degrees is followed by many good salespeople. BUt major
step comes next, and it is misunderstood by too many. It involves educating the prospect.

What the educating prospect mean? As an educator , it is not the salespeoples' sales job to convince the prospect of how must he he/she knows. Instead, the salesperson
would bring all his/her knowledge to bear on his/her analysis of the prospect's problems, and then present his/her solution in the simplest and least complicated way. It took him/her a long time to realize that most prospects are impressed, not with presentations, but with a salesperson's sale ability to solve this sale suitation problem, pinpoint the problem and offer a solution that can be understood.

On conclusion, training salespeople may not be one important factor to influence any organizations‘ sale growth in success, because nay organizations' successes, they depend on many
different factors influence. Training salespeople sale skill issue, it ensures not a important and prior factor to compare other factors to influence any organizations‘ successes. Hence
any organizations' sale growth success can not only depend on salespeopls‘ sale skillful behaviors or sale performances in order to achieve whether how many products number , it can
increase or decrease. I believe that when ay organizations' products sale number, it can be influenced to increase, it is not only influenced by the improvement of the salespeople
sales skillful factor only. Because any large organizations, they have many different departments, they will need to cooperate to work together closely in order to raise efficiencies . So,

their salespeoples‘ performances are influenced by other departments’ efficiencies in possible. For example, if the organization’s factory workers can not produce enough productds number

in order to supply to its shops to sell their customers‘ increasing demand in short time suddenly. Them it has wasted much time to train its salespeople. The reason concerns its factory

workers whether they are proficient ro know how to manufacture their products in short time. For computer products example, the computer product firm ought not only concern how to train its salespeople sale skills to persuade clients to choose to buy its any computer products in sales department and neglects to concern other departments whether they have any problems, because if this computer company has total 50 different computer shops to sell its computer products in any areas in US. If it neglect to concern whether any one shop has enough computer products stock to prepare to sell every day, whether any one of this 50 computer shops has enough computer product stocks number is supplied to satisfy its computer consumers’ purchase needs , their purchase demand must often change suddenly, so it will feel diffcult to predict whether every shop will have how many at least computer customers number every day. Hence, it will need to enquire all computer shop managers whether how many computers number had sold yesturday in order to evaluate whether its warehouse needs to deliver any computers to its any shop in order to have enough stocks to sell to any customers. Hence, training salespeople sale skill will not the prior problem when one computer company has many number of computer shops in US. However, the another problem will be how to improve its computer manufacturing workers‘ computer installation skills to be proficient. If its computer manufacturing workers are not very proficient and they can not manufacture computers in the most efficient speed every day in order to have enough computers number to deliver to its different computer shops every day. It is more prior important issue to need to solve to compare how to raise its computer salespeople sale skills in unpredictive sudden US computer sale growth suitation. Thus, it explains that why training salespeople sale skill factor must not guarantee to influence any organizations’ long term sale growth succss absolutely.

www.ingramcontent.com/pod-product-compliance
Ingram Content Group UK Ltd.
Pitfield, Milton Keynes, MK11 3LW, UK
UKHW041642190726
13854UKWH00006B/2650